# Contents

Mike McGrath

# C++
# Programming

In easy steps is an imprint of Computer Step
Southfield Road · Southam
Warwickshire CV47 0FB · United Kingdom
www.ineasysteps.com

Third Edition

Notice of Liability
Every effort has been made to ensure that this book contains accurate and current information. However, Computer Step and the author shall not be liable for any loss or damage suffered by readers as a result of any information contained herein.

Trademarks
All trademarks are acknowledged as belonging to their respective companies.

Printed and bound in the United Kingdom

ISBN-13 978-1-84078-352-0
ISBN-10 1-84078-352-4

# Foreword

The examples in this book have been carefully prepared to demonstrate many features of C++. You are encouraged to try out the examples on your own computer to discover the exciting possibilities offered by the C++ programming language. The straightforward descriptions should allow you to easily recreate the examples manually or, if you prefer, you can download an archive containing all the compiled example programs and their source code by following these simple steps:

**1** Open your browser and visit our website at **http://www.ineasysteps.com**

**2** Navigate to the "Resource Center" and choose the "Downloads" section

**3** Find the "From C++ Programming in easy steps, 3rd edition" item in the "Source Code" list, then click on the hyperlink entitled All code examples to download the compressed ZIP archive

**4** Extract the contents of the ZIP archive to any convenient location on your computer – for easy reference these are arranged in sub-folders whose names match each chapter title of this book. The programs are named as described in the book and are located in the appropriate chapter folder of the archive. For example, the **hello** program, described in the first chapter, is located in the chapter folder named **1-Getting started**.

# 1 Getting started

*Welcome to the exciting world of C++ programming. This chapter shows how to create a simple program and demonstrates how to store data in a program.*

# Introduction

C++ is an extension of the C programming language that was first implemented on the UNIX operating system by Dennis Ritchie way back in 1972. C is a flexible programming language that remains popular today and is used on a large number of platforms for everything from microcontrollers to the most advanced scientific systems.

C++ was developed by Dr. Bjarne Stroustrup between 1983-1985 while working at AT&T Bell Labs in New Jersey. He added features to the original C language to produce what he called "C with classes". These classes define programming objects with specific features that transform the procedural nature of C into the object-oriented programming language of C++.

The C programming language was so named as it succeeded an earlier programming language named "B" that had been introduced around 1970. The name "C++" displays some programmers' humor because the programming ++ increment operator denotes that C++ is an extension of the C language.

C++, like C, is not platform-dependent so programs can be created on any operating system. Most illustrations in this book depict output on the Windows operating system purely because it is the most widely used desktop platform. The examples can also be created on other platforms such as Linux or MacOS.

## Why learn C++ programming?

The C++ language is favored by many professional programmers because it allows them to create fast, compact programs that are robust and portable.

Using a modern C++ Integrated Development Environment (IDE), such as Microsoft's Visual C++ Express Edition, the programmer can quickly create complex applications. But to use these tools to greatest effect the programmer must first learn quite a bit about the C++ language itself.

This book is an introduction to programming with C++, giving examples of program code and its output to demonstrate the basics of this powerful language.

Don't forget

The freely available Microsoft Visual C++ Express IDE is used in this book to demonstrate visual programming.

## Should I learn C first?

Opinion is divided on the question of whether it is an advantage to be familiar with C programming before moving on to C++. It would seem logical to learn the original language first in order to understand the larger extended language more readily. However, C++ is not simply a larger version of C as the approach to object oriented programming with C++ is markedly different to the procedural nature of C. It is, therefore, arguably better to learn C++ without previous knowledge of C to avoid confusion.

This book makes no assumption that the reader has previous knowledge of any programming language so it is suitable for the beginner to programming in C++, whether they know C or not.

If you do feel that you would benefit from learning to program in C, before moving on to C++, we recommend you try the examples in "C Programming in easy steps" before reading this book.

## Standardization of C++

As the C++ programming language gained in popularity it was adopted by many programmers around the world as their programming language of choice. Some of these programmers began to add their own extensions to the language so it became necessary to agree upon a precise version of C++ that could be commonly shared internationally by all programmers.

A standard version of C++ was defined by a joint committee of the American National Standards Institute (ANSI) and the Industry Organization for Standardization (ISO). This version is sometimes known as ANSI C++ and is portable to any platform and to any development environment.

The examples given in this book conform to ANSI C++. Example programs run in a console window, such as the Command Prompt window on Windows systems or a shell terminal window on Linux systems, to demonstrate the mechanics of the C++ language itself. An example in the final chapter illustrates how code generated automatically by a visual development tool on the Windows platform can, once you're familiar with the C++ language, be edited to create a graphical windowed application.

Hot tip

"ISO" is not an acronym but is derived from the Greek word "isos" meaning "equal" – as in "isometric".

# Installing a compiler

C++ programs are initially created as plain text files, saved with the file extension of ".cpp". These can be written in any text editor, such as Windows' Notepad application or the Vi editor on Linux.

In order to execute a C++ program it must first be "compiled" into byte code that can be understood by the computer. A C++ compiler reads the text version of the program and translates it into a second file – in machine-readable executable format.

Should the text program contain any syntax errors these will be reported by the compiler and the executable file will not be built.

If you are using the Windows platform and have a C++ Integrated Development Environment (IDE) installed then you will already have a C++ compiler available as the compiler is an integral part of the visual IDE. The excellent free Microsoft Visual C++ Express IDE provides an editor window where the program code can be written, and buttons to compile and execute the program. Visual IDEs can, however, seem unwieldy when starting out with C++ because they always create a large number of "project" files that are used by advanced programs.

The popular GNU C++ compiler is available free under the terms of the General Public License (GPL). It is included with most distributions of the Linux operating system. The GNU C++ compiler is also available for Windows platforms and is used to compile examples throughout this book.

To discover if you already have the GNU C++ compiler on your system type **c++ -v** at a command prompt then hit Return. If it's available the compiler will respond with version information. If you are using the Linux platform and the GNU C++ compiler is not available on your computer install it from the distribution disc, or online, or ask your system administrator to install it.

The GNU (pronounced "guh-new") Project was launched back in 1984 to develop a complete free Unix-like operating system. Part of GNU is "Minimalist GNU for Windows" (MinGW). MinGW includes the GNU C++ compiler that can be used on Windows systems to create executable C++ programs. Windows users can download and install the GNU C++ compiler by following the instructions on the opposite page.

The terms and conditions of the General Public License can be found online at **www.gnu.org/copyleft/gpl.html**

**1** With an internet connection, launch a web browser then navigate to **http://sourceforge.net/projects/mingw** and click the "Download MinGW" button to open a packages list

**2** From the list of available packages, click the "Download" button against the Automated MinGW Installer package

| Package | Release | Notes / Monitor | Downloads |
|---------|---------|-----------------|-----------|
| Automated MinGW Installer | MinGW-5.1.3 | 📋 - ✉ | Download |

**3** Download the latest installer file (named something like MinGW-xxx.exe) to your desktop, then launch the installer and choose "Download and Install", "Current"

**4** In the Choose Components dialog, select both the "MinGW base tools" and "g++ compiler" components, then opt to install at the suggested location of **C:\MinGW**

**5** When installation completes, click the System icon in Control Panel then the Advanced System Settings item – to launch the System Properties dialog

**6** In the System Properties dialog, push the Environment Variables button, select the Path System Variable, then push the Edit button and add the location **C:\MinGW\bin** to the Path statement

**7** Click OK to close each dialog, then open a Command Prompt window and enter the command **c++** . If the installation is successful the compiler should respond that you have not specified any input files for compilation

```
Command Prompt                                    _ □ ×
C:\MyPrograms>c++
c++: no input files

C:\MyPrograms>_
```

**Beware**

This installation guide is correct at the time of writing but the procedure is subject to change. Current download information and installation guidance can be found online at **www.mingw.org/download.shtml**.

11

**Don't forget**

Locations in the Path statement are separated by a semi-colon.

# Writing a first C++ program

Follow these steps, copying the code exactly as it is listed, to create a simple C++ program that will output the traditional first program greeting:

hello.cpp

**1** Open a plain text editor, like Notepad, then type these "preprocessor directives"
**#include <iostream>**
**using namespace std ;**

**2** A few lines below preprocessor directives, add a "comment" describing the program
// A C++ Program to output a greeting.

**3** Below the comment, add a "main function" declaration to contain the program statements
**int main()**
**{**

**}**

**4** Between the curly brackets (braces) of the main function, insert this output "statement"
**cout << "Hello World!" << endl ;**

**5** Next insert a final "return" statement in the main function
**return 0 ;**

**6** Save the program to any convenient location as "hello.cpp"- the complete program should look like this:

### Don't forget

Comments throughout this book are shown in green – to differentiate them from other code.

### Beware

After typing the final closing } brace of the main method always hit Return to add a newline character – your compiler may insist that a source file should end with a newline character.

```
hello.cpp - Notepad
File  Edit  Format  View  Help
#include <iostream>
using namespace std ;

// A C++ Program to output a greeting.

int main()
{
        cout << "Hello World!" << endl ;
        return 0 ;
}
```

The separate parts of the program code on the opposite page can be examined individually to understand each part more clearly:

- **Preprocessor Directives** – these are processed by the compiler before the program code so must always appear at the start of the page. Here the **#include** instructs the compiler to use the standard C++ input/output library named **iostream**, specifying the library name between **< >** angled brackets. The next line is the "using directive" that allows functions in the specified namespace to be used without their namespace prefix. Functions of the **iostream** library are within the **std** namespace – so this **using** directive allows functions such as **std::cout** and **std::endl** to be simply written as **cout** and **endl**.

- **Comments** – these should be used to make the code more easily understood by others, and by yourself when revisiting the code later. In C++ programming everything on a single line after a **//** double-slash is ignored by the compiler.

- **Main function** – this is the mandatory entry point of every C++ program. Programs may contain many functions but they must always contain one named **main,** otherwise the compiler will not compile the program. Optionally the parentheses after the function name may specify a comma-separated list of "argument" values to be used by that function. Following execution the function must return a value to the operating system of the data type specified in its declaration – in this case an **int** (integer) value.

- **Statements** – these are the actions that the program will execute when it runs. Each statement must be terminated by a semi-colon, in the same way that English language sentences must be terminated by a full stop period. Here the first statement calls upon the **cout** library function to output text and an **endl** carriage return. These are directed to standard output by the **<<** output stream operator. Notice that text strings in C++ must always be enclosed within double quotes. The final statement employs the C++ **return** keyword to return a zero integer value to the operating system – as required by the main function declaration. Traditionally returning a zero value indicates that the program executed successfully.

**Hot tip**

The C++ compiler also supports multiple-line C-style comments between /* and */ – but these should only ever be used in C++ programming to "comment-out" sections of code when debugging.

**Hot tip**

Notice how the program code is formatted using spacing and indentation (collectively known as whitespace) to improve readability. All whitespace is ignored by the C++ compiler.

# Compiling & running programs

The C++ source code files for the examples in this book are stored in a directory created expressly for that purpose. The directory is named "MyPrograms" – its absolute address on a Windows system is **C:\MyPrograms** and on Linux it's **/home/*user*/MyPrograms**. You can recreate this directory to store programs awaiting compilation:

1   Move the "hello.cpp" program source code file, created on page 12, to the "MyPrograms" directory on your system

2   At a command prompt, use the "cd" command to navigate to the "MyPrograms" directory

3   Enter a command to attempt to compile the program
    **c++ hello.cpp**

When the attempt succeeds the compiler creates an executable file alongside the original source code file. By default the executable file is named **a.exe** on Windows systems and **a.out** on Linux. Compiling a different source code file in the same directory would now overwrite the first executable file without warning. This is obviously undesirable so a custom name for the executable file should be specified when compiling programs, using the compiler's **-o** option in the compile command.

4   Enter a command to compile the program, creating an executable file named "hello.exe" alongside the source file
    **c++ hello.cpp -o hello.exe**

**Hot tip**

At a prompt, enter **c++ --help** to see a list of all compiler options.

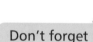

**Don't forget**

The command **c++** is an alias for the GNU C++ compiler – the command **g++** can also be used.

**5** To run the generated executable program file in Windows simply enter the file name at the prompt in the "MyPrograms" directory – optionally the file extension may be omitted. In Linux the full file name must by used, preceded by a ./ dot-slash – as Linux does not look in the current directory unless it is explicitly directed to do so:

**Beware**

All command line examples in this book have been compiled and tested with the GNU C++ compiler (4.1.3) and with the Microsoft C++ compiler from Visual C++ 9.0 – they may not replicate exactly with other compilers.

**Hot tip**

If compilation fails with a message stating "cannot exec cc1plus" search the MinGW directory for **cc1.exe** and **cc1plus.exe** and copy both files into **C:\MinGW\bin** and retry.

# Creating variables

A "variable" is like a container in a C++ program in which a data value can be stored inside the computer's memory. The stored value can be referenced using the variable's name.

The programmer can choose any name for a variable providing it adheres to the C++ naming conventions – a chosen name may only contain letters, digits, and the underscore character, but cannot begin with a digit. Also the C++ keywords, listed on the inside cover of this book, must be avoided. It's good practice to choose meaningful names to make the code more comprehensible.

To create a new variable in a program it must be "declared", specifying the type of data it may contain and its chosen name. A variable declaration has this syntax:

**data-type variable-name ;**

Multiple variables of the same data type can be created in a single declaration as a comma-separated list with this syntax:

**data-type variable-name1 , variable-name2 , variable-name3 ;**

The five basic C++ data types are listed in the table below, together with a brief description and example content:

| Data type | Description | Example |
|-----------|-------------|---------|
| **char** | a single byte, capable of holding one character | 'A' |
| **int** | an integer whole number | 100 |
| **float** | a floating-point number, correct to six decimal places | 0.123456 |
| **double** | a floating-point number, correct to ten decimal places | 0.0123456789 |
| **bool** | a boolean value of **true** or **false**, or numerically zero is false and any non-zero is true | false (0) true (1) |

Variable declarations must appear before executable statements – so they will be available for reference within statements.

**Beware**

Names are case-sensitive in C++ – so variables named **VAR**, **Var**, and **var** are treated as three individual variables. Traditionally C++ variable names are lowercase and seldom begin with an underscore as some C++ libraries use that convention.

**Beware**

Character values of the **char** data type must always be enclosed between single quotes – not double quotes.

When a value is assigned to a variable it is said to have been "initialized". Optionally a variable may be initialized in its declaration. The value stored in any initialized variable can be displayed on standard output by the **cout** function, which was used on page 12 to display the "Hello World!" greeting.

1. Start a new program by specifying the C++ library classes to include and a namespace prefix to use
```
#include <iostream>
using namespace std ;
```

vars.cpp

2. Add a main function containing a final return statement
```
int main()
{
  // Program code goes here.
  return 0 ;
}
```

3. In the main function, insert statements to declare and initialize variables of various data types
```
char letter ;      letter = 'A' ;    // Declared then initialized.
int number ;       number = 100 ;    // Declared then initialized.
float decimal = 7.5 ;                // Declared and initialized.
double pi = 3.14159 ;                // Declared and initialized.
bool isTrue = false ;                // Declared and initialized.
```

4. Now insert statements to output each stored value
```
cout << "char letter: "  << letter << endl ;
cout << "int number: " << number << endl ;
cout << "float decimal: " << decimal << endl ;
cout << "double pi: "  << pi << endl ;
cout << "bool isTrue: " << isTrue << endl ;
```

5. Save, compile, and run the program to see the output

```
Command Prompt                                    _ □ ×

C:\MyPrograms>c++ vars.cpp -o vars.exe

C:\MyPrograms>vars
char letter: A
int number: 100
float decimal: 7.5
double pi: 3.14159
bool isTrue: 0
```

17

Hot tip

Always begin boolean variable names with "is" so they are instantly recognizable as booleans. Also, use "lowerCamelCase" for all variable names that comprise multiple words – where all except the first word begin with uppercase, like "isTrue".

# Employing variable arrays

An array is a variable that can store multiple items of data – unlike a regular array, which can only store one piece of data. The pieces of data are stored sequentially in array "elements" that are numbered, starting at zero. So the first value is stored in element zero, the second value is stored in element one, and so on.

An array is declared in the same way as other variables but additionally the size of the array must also be specified in the declaration, in square brackets following the array name. For example, the syntax to declare a "nums" array to store six integer numbers looks like this:

**int nums[6] ;**

Optionally an array can be initialized when it is declared by assigning values to each element as a comma-separated list enclosed by curly brackets (braces). For example:

**int nums[6] = { 0, 1, 2, 3, 4, 5 } ;**

An individual element can be referenced using the array name followed by square brackets containing the element number. This means that **nums[1]** references the second element in the example above – not the first element, as element numbering starts at zero.

Arrays can be created for any C++ data type, but each element may only contain data of the same data type. An array of characters can be used to store a string of text if the final element contains the special **\0** null character. For example:

**char name[5] = { 'm', 'i', 'k', 'e', '\0' } ;**

The entire string to be referenced just by the array name. This is the principle means of working with strings in the C language but the C++ string class, introduced in chapter four, is far simpler.

Collectively the elements of an array are known as an "index". Arrays can have more than one index – to represent multiple dimensions, rather than the single dimension of a regular array. Multi-dimensional arrays of three indices and more are uncommon, but two-dimensional arrays are useful to store grid-based information, such as coordinates. For example:

**int coords[2] [3] = { { 1, 2, 3 } , { 4, 5, 6 } } ;**

**Don't forget**

Array numbering starts at zero – so the final element in an array of six elements is number five, not number six.

|   | 0 | 1 | 2 |
|---|---|---|---|
| 0 | 1 | 2 | 3 |
| 1 | 4 | 5 | 6 |

1. Start a new program by specifying the C++ library classes to include and a namespace prefix to use

```
#include <iostream>
using namespace std ;
```

arrays.cpp

2. Add a main function containing a final return statement

```
int main()
{
  // Program code goes here.
  return 0 ;
}
```

**Beware**

Where possible variable names should not be abbreviations – abbreviated names are only used in this book's examples due to space limitations.

3. In the main function, insert statements to declare and initialize three variable arrays

```
// Declared then initialized.
float nums[3] ;
nums[0] = 1.5 ; nums[1] = 2.75 ; nums[2] = 3.25 ;

// Declared and initialized.
char name[5] = { 'm', 'i', 'k', 'e', '\0' } ;
int coords[2] [3] = { { 1, 2, 3 } , { 4, 5, 6 } } ;
}
```

4. Now insert statements to output specific element values

```
cout << "nums[0]: " << nums[0] << endl ;
cout << "nums[1]: " << nums[1] << endl ;
cout << "nums[2]: " << nums[2] << endl ;
cout << "name[0]: " << name[0] << endl ;
cout << "string: " << name << endl ;
cout << "coords[0][2]: " << coords[0][2] << endl ;
cout << "coords[1][2]: " << coords[1][2] << endl ;
```

**Hot tip**

The loop structures, introduced in chapter three, are often used to iterate array elements.

5. Save, compile, and run the program to see the output

```
C:\MyPrograms>c++ arrays.cpp -o arrays.exe

C:\MyPrograms>arrays
nums[0]: 1.5
nums[1]: 2.75
nums[2]: 3.25
name[0]: m
Text string: mike
coords[0][2]: 3
coords[1][2]: 6

C:\MyPrograms>_
```
Command Prompt

# Employing vector arrays

A vector is an alternative to a regular array and has the advantage that its size can be changed as the program requires. Like regular arrays, vectors can be created for any data type and their elements are also numbered starting at zero.

In order to use vectors in a program the C++ **vector** library must be added with an **#include <vector>** preprocessor directive at the start of the program. This library contains the predefined functions in the table below, which are used to work with vectors:

| Function | Description |
| --- | --- |
| **at(** element number **)** | gets the value contained in the specified element |
| **back()** | gets the value in the final element |
| **clear()** | removes all vector elements |
| **empty()** | returns true (1) if the vector is empty, or returns false (0) otherwise |
| **front()** | gets the value in the first element |
| **pop_back()** | removes the final element |
| **push_back(** value **)** | adds an element to the end of the vector, containing the specified value |
| **size()** | gets the number of elements |

A declaration to create a vector looks like this:

**vector < *data-type* > *vector-name* ( *size* ) ;**

An **int** vector will, by default have each element automatically initialized with a zero value. Optionally a different initial value can be specified after the size in the declaration with this syntax:

**vector < *data-type* > *vector-name* ( *size* , *initial-value* ) ;**

The functions to work with vectors are simply appended to the chosen vector name by the dot operator. For example, to get the size of a vector named "vec" you would use **vec.size()** .

**Don't forget**

Individual vector elements can be referenced using square brackets as with regular arrays, such as **vec[3]**.

**1** Start a new program by specifying the C++ library classes to include and a namespace prefix to use

```cpp
#include <vector>              // Include vector support.
#include <iostream>
using namespace std ;
```

vector.cpp

**2** Add a main function containing a final return statement

```cpp
int main()
{
  // Program code goes here.
  return 0 ;
}
```

**3** In the main function, insert a statement to declare and initialize a vector array of three elements of the value 100

```cpp
vector <int> vec( 3, 100 ) ;
```

**4** Now insert statements to manipulate the vector elements

```cpp
cout << "Vector size: " << vec.size() << endl ;
cout << "Is empty?: " << vec.empty() << endl ;
cout << "First element: " << vec.at(0) << endl ;

vec.pop_back() ;           // Remove final element.
cout << "Vector size: " << vec.size() << endl ;
cout << "Final element: " << vec.back() << endl;

vec.clear() ;              // Remove all elements.
cout << "Vector size: " << vec.size() << endl;

vec.push_back( 200 ) ;  // Add an element.
cout << "Vector size: " << vec.size() << endl ;
cout << "First element: " << vec.front() << endl ;
```

**5** Save, compile, and run the program to see the output

```
Command Prompt                                    _ □ X

C:\MyPrograms>c++ vector.cpp -o vector.exe

C:\MyPrograms>vector
Vector size: 3
Is empty?: 0
First element: 100
Vector size: 2
Final element: 100
Vector size: 0
Vector size: 1
First element: 200
```

21

Hot tip

The example on page 50 shows how to use a loop to populate a vector with different initial values in each element.

# Declaring constants

Data that will not change during the execution of a program should be stored in a constant container, rather than in a variable. This better enables the compiler to check the code for errors – if the program attempts to change the value stored in a constant the compiler will report an error and the compilation will fail.

A constant can be created for any data type by prefixing a variable declaration with the **const** keyword, followed by a space. Typically constant names appear in uppercase to distinguish them from (lowercase) variable names. Unlike variables, constants must always be initialized in the declaration. For example, the declaration of a constant for the math pi value looks like this:

**const double PI = 3.1415926536 ;**

The **enum** keyword provides a handy way to create a sequence of integer constants in a concise manner. Optionally, the declaration can include a name for the sequence after the **enum** keyword. The constant names follow as a comma-separated list within braces. For example, this declaration creates a sequence of constants:

**enum suit { CLUBS , DIAMONDS , HEARTS , SPADES } ;**

Each of the constants will, by default, have a value one greater than the preceding constant in the list. Unless specified the first constant will have a value of zero, the next a value of one, and so on. A constant can be assigned any integer value but the next constant in the list will always increment it by one.

**Don't forget**

The **typedef** keyword simply creates a nickname for a structure.

It is occasionally convenient to define a list of enumerated constants as a "custom data type" – by using the **typedef** keyword. This can begin the **enum** declaration and a chosen type name can be added at the end of the declaration. For example, this **typedef** statement creates a custom data type named "charge":

**typedef enum { NEGATIVE , POSITIVE } charge ;**

Variables can then be created of the custom data type in the usual way, which may legally be assigned any of the listed constants. Essentially these variables act just like an **int** variable – as they store the numerical integer value the assigned constant represents. For example, with the example above, assigning a **POSITIVE** constant to a **charge** variable actually assigns an integer of one.

1　Start a new program by specifying the C++ library classes to include and a namespace prefix to use

```
#include <iostream>
using namespace std ;
```

constant.cpp

2　Add a main function containing a final return statement

```
int main()
{
  // Program code goes here.
  return 0 ;
}
```

3　In the main function, insert statements to declare a constant and output using the constant value

```
const double PI = 3.1415926536 ;
cout << "6\" circle circumference: " << (PI * 6) << endl ;
```

4　Next insert statements to declare an enumerated list of constants and output using some of those constant values

```
enum
{ RED=1, YELLOW, GREEN, BROWN, BLUE, PINK, BLACK } ;
cout << "I shot a red worth: " << RED << endl ;
cout << "Then a blue worth: " << BLUE << endl ;
cout << "Total scored: " << ( RED + BLUE ) << endl ;
```

5　Now insert statements to declare a custom data type and output its assigned values

```
typedef enum { NEGATIVE , POSITIVE } charge ;
charge neutral = NEGATIVE , live = POSITIVE ;
cout << "Neutral wire: " << neutral << endl ;
cout << "Live wire: " << live << endl ;
```

6　Save, compile, and run the program to see the output

```
Command Prompt                                        _ □ ×

C:\MyPrograms>c++ constant.cpp -o constant.exe

C:\MyPrograms>constant
6" circle circumference: 18.8496
I shot a red worth: 1
Then a blue worth: 5
Total scored: 6
Neutral wire: 0
Live wire: 1

C:\MyPrograms>_
```

Hot tip

In the PI declaration the * character is the C++ multiplication operator, and the backslash character in \" escapes the quote mark from recognition – so the string does not get terminated prematurely.

# Summary

- C++ is an object-oriented programming language that is an extension of the procedural C programming language

- The GNU C++ compiler is available for Windows and Linux

- Preprocessor instructions are used to make functions within the standard C++ libraries available to a program

- Each C++ program must contain one main method as the entry point to the program

- Statements define the actions that the program will execute

- It is recommended that program code should be widely commented to make its purpose clear

- The **c++** command calls the compiler and its **-o** option allows the command to specify the name of the generated executable

- A variable declaration specifies a data type and a chosen name by which the value within that variable can be referenced

- The **cout** function, which is part of the C++ **iostream** library, writes content to the standard output console

- An array is a fixed size variable that stores multiple items of data in elements, which are numbered starting at zero

- The special **\0** character can be assigned to the final element of a **char** array to allow it to be treated as a single text string

- A vector variable stores multiple items of data in elements and can be dynamically resized

- The value stored in an array or vector element can be referenced using that variable's name and its index number

- Variable values that are never changed by the program should be stored in a constant

- A constant list can be automatically numbered by the **enum** keyword and given a type name by the **typedef** keyword

# 2 Performing operations

*This chapter introduces the C++ operators and demonstrates the operations they can perform.*

# Doing arithmetic

The arithmetical operators commonly used in C++ programs are listed in the table below together with the operation they perform:

| Operator | Operation |
|:---:|:---|
| + | Addition |
| - | Subtraction |
| * | Multiplication |
| / | Division |
| % | Modulus |
| ++ | Increment |
| -- | Decrement |

The operators for addition, subtraction, multiplication, and division act as you would expect. Care must be taken, however, to bracket expressions where more than one operator is used to clarify the expression – operations within innermost parentheses are performed first:

**a = b * c - d % e / f ;**          // This is unclear.

**a = ( b * c ) - ( ( d % e ) / f ) ;**          // This is clearer.

The **%** modulus operator will divide the first given number by the second given number and return the remainder of the operation. This is useful to determine if a number has an odd or even value.

The **++** increment operator and -- decrement operator alter the given number by one and return the resulting value. These are most commonly used to count iterations in a loop. Counting up, the **++** operator increases the value by one while, counting down, the -- decrement operator decreases the value by one.

The increment and decrement operators can be placed before or after a value to different effect. If placed before the operand (prefix) its value is immediately changed, if placed after the operand (postfix) its value is noted first, then the value is changed.

The difference between placing the increment operator before and after an **int** variable is demonstrated in the program opposite.

### Hot tip

Values used with operators to form expressions are called "operands" – in the expression **2 + 3** the numerical values **2** and **3** are the operands.

① Start a new program by specifying the C++ library classes to include and a namespace prefix to use

```
#include <iostream>
using namespace std ;
```

arithmetic.cpp

② Add a main function containing a final return statement

```
int main()
{
  // Program code goes here.
  return 0 ;
}
```

③ In the main function, insert a statement to declare and initialize two integer variables

```
int a = 8 , b = 4 ;
```

④ Next insert statements to output the result of each basic arithmetic operation

```
cout << "Addition result: "       << ( a + b ) << endl ;
cout << "Subtraction result: "    << ( a - b ) << endl ;
cout << "Multiplication result: " << ( a * b ) << endl ;
cout << "Division result: "       << ( a / b ) << endl ;
cout << "Modulus result: "        << ( a % b ) << endl ;
```

⑤ Now insert statements to output the result of both postfix and prefix increment operations

```
cout << "Postfix increment: "  << a++ << endl ;
cout << "Postfix result: "     << a << endl ;
cout << "Prefix increment: "   << ++b << endl ;
cout << "Prefix result: "      << b << endl ;
```

⑥ Save, compile, and run the program to see the output

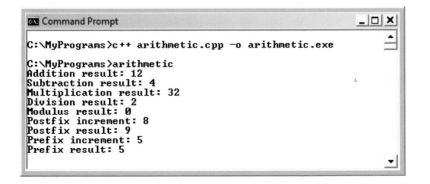

27

**Don't forget**

Remember that a prefix operator changes the variable value immediately – a postfix operator changes the value subsequently.

# Assigning values

The operators that are used in C++ programming to assign values are listed in the table below. All except the simple = assignment operator are a shorthand form of a longer expression so each equivalent is given for clarity:

| Operator | Example | Equivalent |
|:---:|:---|:---|
| = | a = b | a = b |
| += | a += b | a = ( a + b ) |
| -= | a -= b | a = ( a - b ) |
| *= | a *= b | a = ( a * b ) |
| /= | a /= b | a = ( a / b ) |
| %= | a %= b | a = ( a % b ) |

It is important to regard the = operator to mean "assign" rather than "equals" to avoid confusion with the == equality operator.

In the example above the variable named "a" is assigned the value that is contained in the variable named "b" – so that becomes the new value stored in the **a** variable.

The **+=** operator is useful to add a value onto an existing value that is stored in the **a** variable.

In the table example the **+=** operator first adds the value contained in variable **a** to the value contained in variable **b**. It then assigns the result to become the new value stored in variable **a**.

All the other operators work in the same way by making the arithmetical operation between the two values first, then assigning the result of that operation to the first variable – to become its new stored value.

With the **%=** operator the first operand **a** is divided by the second operand **b** then the remainder of that operation is assigned to the **a** variable.

Each assignment operation is demonstrated in the program on the opposite page.

**Beware**

The == equality operator compares operands and is described on page 30.

**1** Start a new program by specifying the C++ library classes to include and a namespace prefix to use
```
#include <iostream>
using namespace std ;
```

assign.cpp

**2** Add a main function containing a final return statement
```
int main()
{
  // Program code goes here.
  return 0 ;
}
```

**3** In the main function, insert a statement declaring two integer variables
```
int a , b ;
```

**4** Next insert statements to output simple assigned values
```
cout << "Assign values: " ;
cout << "a = " << ( a = 8 ) << "   " ;
cout << "b = " << ( b = 4 ) ;
```

**5** Now insert statements to output combined assigned values
```
cout << endl << "Add & assign: " ;
cout << "a += b (8 += 4 ) a = " << ( a += b ) ;
cout << endl << "Subtract & assign: " ;
cout << "a -= b (12 -= 4 ) a = " << ( a -= b ) ;
cout << endl << "Multiply & assign: " ;
cout << "a *= b (8 *= 4 ) a = " << ( a *= b ) ;
cout << endl << "Divide & assign: " ;
cout << "a /= b (32 /= 4 ) a = " << ( a /= b ) ;
cout << endl << "Modulus & assign: " ;
cout << "a %= b (8 %= 4 )  a = " << ( a %= b ) ;
```

**6** Save, compile, and run the program to see the output

29

**Hot tip**

Notice how the **\n** newline escape sequence is used here for carriage returns in place of **endl**.

```
Command Prompt                                    _ □ X

C:\MyPrograms>c++ assign.cpp -o assign.exe

C:\MyPrograms>assign
Assign values:  a = 8    b = 4
Add & assign:  a += b (8 += 4 ) a = 12
Subtract & assign: a -= b (12 -= 4 ) a = 8
Multiply & assign: a *= b (8 *= 4 ) a = 32
Divide & assign: a /= b (32 /= 4 ) a = 8
Modulus & assign: a %= b (8 %= 4 )  a = 0
```

# Comparing values

The operators that are commonly used in C++ programming to compare two numerical values are listed in the table below:

| Operator | Comparative test |
|:---:|---|
| == | Equality |
| != | Inequality |
| > | Greater than |
| < | Less than |
| >= | Greater than or equal to |
| <= | Less than or equal to |

The == equality operator compares two operands and will return **true** (1) if both are equal in value, otherwise it will return a **false** (0) value. If both are the same number they are equal, or if both are characters their ASCII code values are compared numerically.

Conversely the != inequality operator returns **true** (1) if two operands are not equal, using the same rules as the == equality operator, otherwise it returns **false** (0).

Equality and inequality operators are useful in testing the state of two variables to perform conditional branching in a program.

The > "greater than" operator compares two operands and will return **true** (1) if the first is greater in value than the second, or it will return **false** (0) if it is equal or less in value. The > "greater than" operator is often used to test the value of a countdown value in a loop. The < "less than" operator makes the same comparison but returns **true** (1) if the first operand is less in value than the second, otherwise it returns **false** (0).

Adding the = operator after a > "greater than" or < "less than" operator makes it also return **true** (1) if the two operands are exactly equal in value.

Each comparison operation is demonstrated in the program on the opposite page.

**Hot tip**

A-Z uppercase characters have ASCII code values 65-90 and a-z lowercase characters have ASCII code values 97-122.

**1** Start a new program by specifying the C++ library classes to include and a namespace prefix to use

```
#include <iostream>
using namespace std ;
```

comparison.cpp

**2** Add a main function containing a final return statement

```
int main()
{
  // Program code goes here.
  return 0 ;
}
```

**3** In the main function, insert statements to declare and initialize variables that can convert to booleans

```
int nil = 0, num = 0, max = 1 ; char cap = 'A', low = 'a' ;
```

**4** Next insert statements to output equality comparisons of integers and characters

```
cout << "Equality comparisons: " ;
cout << "(0 == 0) " << ( nil == num ) << "(true)  " ;
cout << "(A == a) " << (cap == low) << "(false)";
```

**5** Now insert statements to output all other comparisons

```
cout << endl << "Inequality comparison: " ;
cout << "(0 != 1) " << ( nil != max )    << "(true)" ;
cout << endl << "Greater comparison: " ;
cout << "(0 > 1) " << ( nil > max )       << "(false)"
cout << endl << "Lesser comparison: " ;
cout << "(0 < 1) " << ( nil < max )       << "(true)" ;
cout << endl << "Greater or equal comparison: " ;
cout << "(0 >= 0) "<< ( nil >= num ) << "(true)" ;
cout << endl << "Lesser or equal comparison: " ;
cout << "(1 <= 0) " << ( max <= num ) << "(false)" ;
```

**Don't forget**

The ASCII code value for uppercase "A" is 65 but for lowercase "a" it's 97 – so their comparison here returns **false** (0).

**6** Save, compile, and run the program to see the output

```
Command Prompt                                            _ □ X
C:\MyPrograms>c++ comparison.cpp -o comparison.exe          ▲
C:\MyPrograms>comparison
Equality comparisons: (0 == 0) 1(true)  (A == a) 0(false)
Inequality comparison:  (0 != 1) 1(true)
Greater comparison:   (0 > 1) 0(false)
Lesser comparison:   (0 < 1) 1(true)
Greater or equal comparison: (0 >= 0) 1(true)
Lesser or equal comparison: (1 <= 0) 0(false)             ▼
```

# Assessing logic

The logical operators most commonly used in C++ programming are listed in the table below:

| Operator | Operation |
|---|---|
| && | Logical AND |
| \|\| | Logical OR |
| ! | Logical NOT |

The logical operators are used with operands that have boolean values of **true** or **false**, or are values that convert to **true** or **false**.

The logical **&&** AND operator will evaluate two operands and return **true** only if both operands themselves are **true**. Otherwise the **&&** operator will return **false**.

This is used in conditional branching where the direction of a program is determined by testing two conditions. If both conditions are satisfied the program will go in a certain direction, otherwise it will take a different direction.

Unlike the **&&** AND operator that needs both operands to be **true** the **||** OR operator will evaluate its two operands and return **true** if either one of the operands itself returns **true**. If neither operand returns **true** then the **||** OR operator will return **false**. This is useful in C++ programming to perform a certain action if either one of two test conditions has been met.

The third logical **!** NOT operator is a unary operator that is used before a single operand. It returns the inverse value of the given operand so if the variable **a** had a value of **true** then **!a** would have a value of **false**. The **!** NOT operator is useful in C++ programs to toggle the value of a variable in successive loop iterations with a statement like **a = !a**. This ensures that on each pass the value is changed, like flicking a light switch on and off.

In C++ programs a zero represents the boolean **false** value and any non-zero value, such as one, represents the boolean **true** value.

Each logical operation is demonstrated in the program on the opposite page.

## Beware

Where there is more than one operand each expression must be enclosed by parentheses.

## Hot tip

The term "boolean" refers to a system of logical thought developed by the English mathematician George Boole (1815-1864).

1. Start a new program by specifying the C++ library classes to include and a namespace prefix to use
```
#include <iostream>
using namespace std ;
```

logic.cpp

2. Add a main function containing a final return statement
```
int main()
{
  // Program code goes here.
  return 0 ;
}
```

3. In the main function, declare and initialize two integer variables – with values that can represent boolean values
```
int a = 1 , b = 0 ;
```

4. Insert statements to output the result of AND evaluations
```
cout << "AND logic:" << endl ;
cout << "(a && a) " << (a && a) << "(true) " ;
cout << "(a && b) " << (a && b) << "(false) " ;
cout << "(b && b) " << (b && b) << "(false)" << endl ;
```

5. Insert statements to output the result of OR evaluations
```
cout << endl << "OR logic:" << endl ;
cout << "(a || a) " << (a || a) << "(true) " ;
cout << "(a || b) " << (a || b) << "(true) ";
cout << "(b || b) " << (b || b) << "(false)" << endl ;
```

6. Insert statements to output the result of NOT evaluations
```
cout << endl << "NOT logic:" << endl ;
cout << "a = " << a << " !a = " << !a << "   " ;
cout << "b = " << b << " !b = " << !b << endl ;
```

7. Save, compile, and run the program to see the output

```
 Command Prompt                                    _ □ ×
C:\MyPrograms>c++ logic.cpp -o logic.exe

C:\MyPrograms>logic
AND logic:
(a && a) 1(true)  (a && b) 0(false)  (b && b) 0(false)
OR  logic:
(a || a) 1(true)  (a || b) 1(true)  (b || b) 0(false)
NOT logic:
a = 1  !a= 0  b = 0  !b= 1
```

33

**Don't forget**

Notice that 0 && 0 returns 0, not 1 – demonstrating the maxim that two wrongs don't make a right.

# Examining conditions

Possibly the C++ programmer's most favorite test operator is the ?: "ternary" operator. This operator first evaluates an expression for a **true** or **false** condition then returns one of two specified values depending on the result of the evaluation. For this reason it is also known as the "conditional" operator.

The ?: ternary operator has this syntax:

( *test-expression* ) ? *if-true-return-this* : *if-false-return-this* ;

Although the ternary operator can initially appear a little confusing it is well worth becoming familiar with this operator as it can execute powerful program branching with minimal code. For example, to branch when a variable is not a value of one:

( *var* != 1 ) ? *if-true-do-this* : *if-false-do-this* ;

The ternary operator is commonly used in C++ programming to assign the maximum, or minimum, value of two variables to a third variable. For example, to assign a minimum like this:

**c = ( a < b ) ? a : b ;**

The expression in parentheses returns **true** when the value of variable **a** is less than that of variable **b** – so, in this case, the lesser value of variable **a** gets assigned to variable **c**.

Similarly, replacing the < less than operator in the test expression with the > greater than operator would assign the greater value of variable **b** to variable **c**.

Another common use of the ternary operator incorporates the **%** modulus operator in the test expression to determine whether the value of a variable is an odd number or an even number:

( *var % 2 != 0* ) ? *if-true(odd)-do-this* : *if-false(even)-do-this* ;

Where the result of dividing the variable value by two does leave a remainder the number is odd – where there is no remainder the number is even. The test expression ( **var % 2 == 1** ) would have the same effect but it is preferable to test for inequality – it's easier to spot when something is different than when it's identical.

The ternary operator is demonstrated in the program on the opposite page.

**Don't forget**

The ternary operator has three operands – the one before the **?**, and those before and after the **:** .

1. Start a new program by specifying the C++ library classes to include and a namespace prefix to use

```
#include <iostream>
using namespace std ;
```

ternary.cpp

2. Add a main function containing a final return statement

```
int main()
{
  // Program code goes here.
  return 0 ;
}
```

3. In the main function, insert statements declaring three integer variables, and initializing two of them

```
int a, b, max ;
a = 1, b = 2 ;
```

4. Insert statements to output the value and parity of the first examined variable

```
cout << "Variable a value is: " ;
cout << ( ( a != 1 ) ? "not one, " : "one, " ) ;
cout << ( ( a % 2 != 0 ) ? "odd" : "even" ) ;
```

5. Next insert statements to output the value and parity of the second examined variable

```
cout << endl << "Variable b value is: " ;
cout << ( ( b != 1 ) ? "not one, " : "one, " ) ;
cout << ( ( b % 2 != 0 ) ? "odd" : "even" ) ;
```

6. Now insert statements to output the greater of the two stored variable values

```
max = ( a > b ) ? a : b ;
cout << endl << "Greater value is: " << max << endl ;
```

7. Save, compile and run the program to see the output

```
Command Prompt                                    _ □ X

C:\MyPrograms>c++ ternary.cpp -o ternary.exe

C:\MyPrograms>ternary
Variable a value is: one, odd
Variable b value is: not one, even
Greater value is: 2
```

**Hot tip**

The ternary operator can return values of any data type – numbers, strings, boolean values, etc..

35

# Establishing size

Declaration of a variable allocates system memory where values assigned to that variable will be stored. The amount of memory allocated for this is determined by your system and the data type.

Typically an **int** data type is created as a "long" value by default, which can store values from +2,147,483,647 to -2,147,483,648. On the other hand, if the **int** data type is created as a "short" value by default it can only store values from +32,767 to -32,768.

The preferred range can be explicitly specified when declaring the variable by prefixing the **int** keyword with a **short** or **long** qualifier. The **short int** is useful to save memory space when you are sure the limited range will never be exceeded.

When an **int** variable is declared it can by default contain either positive or negative integers, which are known as "signed" values. If the variable will always contain only positive integers it can be qualified as **unsigned** to increase its maximum possible value. Typically an **unsigned short int** has a range from zero to 65,535 and an **unsigned long int** has a range from zero to 4,294,967,295.

The memory size of any variable can be discovered using the C++ **sizeof** operator. The name of the variable to be examined can be specified in optional parentheses following the **sizeof** operator name. For example, to examine a variable named "var":

**sizeof( var ) ;**     // Alternatively you can use "sizeof var ;".

The **sizeof** operator will return an integer that is the number of bytes allocated to store data within the named variable.

Simple data types, such as **char** and **bool**, only need a single byte of memory to store just one piece of data. Longer numeric values need more memory, according to their possible range – determined by data type and qualifiers.

The memory allocated to an array is simply a multiple of that allocated to a single variable of its data type, according to its number of elements. For example, an **int** array of 50 elements will allocate fifty times the memory allocated to a single **int** variable.

The **sizeof** operator is demonstrated in the program on the opposite page.

## Hot tip

Although **sizeof** is an operator that does not strictly need parentheses it is commonly seen with them – as if it was a function, like **main()**.

**1** Start a new program by specifying the C++ library classes to include and a namespace prefix to use

```
#include <iostream>
using namespace std ;
```

sizeof.cpp

**2** Add a main function containing a final return statement

```
int main()
{
  // Program code goes here.
  return 0 ;
}
```

**3** In the main function, insert statements declaring variables of various data types

```
int num ;          int nums[50] ;        float decimal ;
bool isTrue ;      unsigned int max ;    char letter ;
double pi ;        short int number ;    char letters[50] ;
```

**4** Next insert statements to output the byte size of each integer variable

```
cout << "int size:" << sizeof( num ) << endl ;
cout << "50 int size: " << sizeof( nums ) << endl ;
cout << "short int size: " << sizeof( number ) << endl ;
cout << "unsigned int size: " << sizeof( max ) << endl ;
```

**5** Now insert statements to output the size of other variables

```
cout << "double size: " << sizeof( pi ) << endl ;
cout << "float size: " << sizeof( decimal ) << endl ;
cout << "char size: " << sizeof( letter ) << endl ;
cout << "50 char size: " << sizeof( letters ) << endl ;
cout << "bool size: " << sizeof( isTrue ) << endl ;
```

**Don't forget**

Here the **int** data type is created as a **long** type by default – your system may be different.

**6** Save, compile and run the program to see the output

```
 Command Prompt                                          _ □ ×
C:\MyPrograms>c++ sizeof.cpp -o sizeof.exe

C:\MyPrograms>sizeof
int size: 4
50 int size: 200
short int size: 2
unsigned int size: 4
double size: 8
float size: 4
char size: 1
50 char size: 50
bool size: 1
```

37

# Setting precedence

Operator precedence determines the order in which C++ evaluates expressions. For example, in the expression **a = 6 + 8 * 3** the order of precedence determines that multiplication is completed first.

The table below lists operator precedence in descending order – those on the top row have highest precedence, those on lower rows have successively lower precedence. The precedence of operators on the same row is determined by their position in the expression, according to the direction listed for that operator.

**Don't forget**

The * multiply operator is on a higher row than the + addition operator – so in the expression **a=6+8*3** multiplication is completed first, before the addition.

| Operator | | | | Direction |
| --- | --- | --- | --- | --- |
| ( ) Function call<br>-> Class pointer | | [ ] Array index<br>. Class member | | Left to right |
| ! Logical NOT<br>-- Decrement<br>+ Positive sign<br>sizeof Size of | | * Pointer<br>++ Increment<br>- Negative sign<br>& Address of | | Right to left |
| * Multiply<br>% Modulus | | / Divide | | Left to right |
| + Add | | - Subtract | | Left to right |
| <= Less or equal<br>>= Greater or equal | | < Less than<br>> Greater than | | Left to right |
| == Equality | | != Inequality | | Left to right |
| && Logical AND | | | | Left to right |
| \|\| Logical OR | | | | Left to right |
| ?: Ternary | | | | Right to left |
| = += -= *= /= %= | | Assignments | | Right to left |
| , Comma | | | | Left to right |

**Hot tip**

The -> class pointer and the . class member operators are introduced later in this book – but they are included here for completeness.

In addition to the operators in this table there are a number of "bitwise" operators, which are used to perform binary arithmetic. This is outside the scope of this book but there is a section devoted to binary arithmetic in "C Programming in easy steps". Those operators perform in just the same way in C++.

Operator precedence is demonstrated in the program opposite.

1. Start a new program by specifying the C++ library classes to include and a namespace prefix to use

```
#include <iostream>
using namespace std ;
```

precedence.cpp

2. Add a main function continuing a final return statement

```
int main()
{
  // Program code goes here.
  return 0 ;
}
```

3. In the main function, declare an integer variable initialized with the result of an expression using default precedence, then output the result

```
num = 1 + 4 * 3;
cout << endl << "Default order: " << num << endl ;
```

4. Next assign the result of this expression to the variable using explicit precedence, then output the result

```
num = ( 1 + 4 ) * 3 ;
cout << "Forced order: " << num << endl << endl ;
```

5. Assign the result of a different expression to the variable using direction precedence, then output the result

```
num = 7 - 4 + 2 ;
cout<< "Default direction: " << num << endl ;
```

6. Now assign the result of this expression to the variable using explicit precedence, then output the result

```
num = 7 - ( 4 + 2 ) ;
cout << "Forced direction: " << num << endl ;
```

7. Save, compile and run the program to see the output

Beware

Do not rely upon default precedence as it may vary between compilers – always use parentheses to clarify expressions.

```
Command Prompt                                    _ □ X
C:\MyPrograms>c++ precedence.cpp -o precedence.exe

C:\MyPrograms>precedence

Default order:  13
Forced order:   15

Default direction: 5
Forced direction: 1
```

# Casting data types

Any data stored in a variable can be forced (coerced) into a variable of a different data type by a process known as "casting". The cast statement simply states the data type to which the value should be cast in parentheses preceding the name of the variable containing the data to be cast. So casting syntax looks like this:

*variable-name* = ( *data-type* ) *variable-name* ;

This is the traditional form of casting that is also found in the C programming language. A newer alternative available in C++ uses angled brackets with the **static_cast** keyword like this:

*variable-name* = static_cast < *data-type* > *variable-name* ;

The newer version allows casts to be more easily identified in source code by avoiding the use of parentheses, which can easily be confused with parentheses in expressions. The newer form of casting is preferred but the older form is still widely found.

Casting is often necessary to accurately store the result of an arithmetic operation because dividing one integer by another integer will always produce an integer result. For example, the integer division **7/2** produces the truncated integer result of **3**.

To store the accurate floating-point result would require the result be cast into a suitable data type, such as a **float**, like this:

**float result = ( float ) 7 / 2 ;**

Or alternatively using the newer form of cast:

**float result = static_cast < float > 7 / 2 ;**

In either case it should be noted that operator precedence casts the first operand into the specified data type before implementing the arithmetic operation, so the statement can best be written as:

**float result = static_cast < float > ( 7 ) / 2 ;**

Bracketing the expression as **( 7 / 2 )** would perform the arithmetic first on integers, so the integer result would be truncated before being cast into the **float** variable – not the desired effect!

Casting with both the older C-style form and the newer C++ form is demonstrated in the program on the opposite page.

1 Start a new program by specifying the C++ library classes to include and a namespace prefix to use
```
#include <iostream>
using namespace std ;
```

cast.cpp

2 Add a main function containing a final return statement
```
int main()
{
  // Program code goes here.
  return 0 ;
}
```

3 In the main function, insert statements to declare and initialize integer, character, and floating-point variables
```
int num = 7, factor = 2 ;
char letter = 'A' ; float result = 0.0 ;
```

4 Output the result of a plain integer division
```
cout << "Integer division: " << ( num / factor ) << endl ;
```

5 Now cast the same division into a floating-point variable and output that result
```
result = (float) (num) / factor ;
cout << "Cast division float: " << result << endl ;
```

6 Next cast a character variable into an integer variable and output that value
```
num = static_cast <int> (letter) ;
cout << "Cast character int: " << num << endl ;
```

7 Cast an integer into a character variable and output it
```
letter = static_cast <char> (70) ;
cout << "Cast integer char: " << letter << endl ;
```

8 Save, compile and run the program to see the output

```
Command Prompt                                    _ □ X
C:\MyPrograms>c++ cast.cpp -o cast.exe

C:\MyPrograms>cast
Integer division: 3
Cast division float: 3.5
Cast character int: 65
Cast integer char: F
```

41

### Hot tip

ASCII (pronounced "askee") is the American Standard Code for Information Interchange, which is the accepted standard for plain text. In ASCII, characters are represented numerically within the range 0-127. Uppercase 'A' is 65 so that integer value gets cast into an **int** variable.

# Summary

- Arithmetical operators can form expressions with two operands for addition **+**, subtraction **-**, multiplication **\***, division **/**, or modulus **%**

- Increment **++** and decrement **--** operators modify a single operand by a value of one

- The assignment **=** operator can be combined with an arithmetical operator to perform an arithmetical calculation then assign its result

- Comparison operators can form expressions comparing two operands for equality **==**, inequality **!=**, greater **>**, lesser **<**, greater or equal **>=**, and lesser or equal **<=** values

- Logical **&&** and **||** operators form expressions evaluating two operands to return a boolean value of true or false

- The logical **!** operator returns the inverse boolean value of a single operand

- A ternary **?:** operator evaluates a given boolean expression then returns one of two operands depending on its result

- The **sizeof** operator returns the memory byte size of a variable

- An **int** variable may be qualified as a **short** type for smaller numbers or as a **long** type for large numbers

- Where an **int** variable will only store positive numbers it may be qualified as **unsigned** to extend its numeric range

- It is important to explicitly set operator precedence in complex expressions by adding parentheses **( )**

- Data stored in a variable can be forced into a variable of a different data type by the casting process

- C++ supports traditional C-style casts and the newer form of casts that use the **static_cast** keyword

# 3 Making statements

This chapter describes the conditional statements, which allow C++ programs to branch in different directions, and introduces function structures.

# Branching with if

The C++ **if** keyword performs the basic conditional test that evaluates a given expression for a boolean value of **true** or **false** – and its syntax looks like this:

**if ( *test-expression* ) { *statements-to-execute-when-true* }**

The braces following the test may contain one or more statements, each terminated by a semi-colon, but these will only be executed when the expression is found to be **true**. When the test is found to be **false** the program proceeds to its next task.

Optionally, an **if** statement can offer alternative statements to execute when the test fails by appending an **else** statement block after the **if** statement block like this:

**if ( *test-expression* ) { *statements-to-execute-when-true* }**
**else { *statements-to-execute-when-false* }**

To test two conditions the test expression may use the **&&** operator. For example, **if ( ( num > 5 ) && ( letter == 'A' ) ).** Alternatively, an **if** statement can be "nested" within another **if** statement, so those statements in the inner statement block will only be executed when both tests succeed – but statements in the outer statement block will be executed if the outer test succeeds.

## Hot tip

When there is only one statement to execute when the test succeeds the braces may be omitted – but retaining them aids code clarity.

44

ifelse.cpp

**1** Start a new program by specifying the C++ library classes to include and a namespace prefix to use
**#include <iostream>**
**using namespace std ;**

**2** Add a main function containing a final return statement
**int main()**
**{**
  **// Program code goes here.**
  **return 0 ;**
**}**

**3** In the main function, insert statements to declare and initialize two variables
**int num = 8 ;**
**char letter = 'A' ;**

4   Next insert an if-else statement that tests the integer
    variable value and outputs an appropriate response
    **if( num > 5 )**
    **{ cout << "Number exceeds five" << endl ;       }**
    **else**
    **{ cout << "Number is five or less" << endl ;       }**

### Hot tip

Shorthand can be used
when testing a boolean
value – so the expression
**if ( flag == true )** can be
written as just **if ( flag )**.

5   In the if statement block, insert a nested if statement that
    tests the character variable value and outputs when matched
    **if( letter == 'A' ) { cout << "Letter is A" << endl ;       }**

6   Save, compile and run the program to see both tests succeed

```
Command Prompt                                    _ □ X
C:\MyPrograms>c++ ifelse.cpp -o ifelse.exe         ▲
C:\MyPrograms>ifelse
Number exceeds five
Letter is A                                        ▼
```

7   Edit the character variable declaration to change its value
    **char letter = 'B' ;**

8   Save, compile, and run the program once more to see only
    the outer test succeed – executing the outer if statement

```
Command Prompt                                    _ □ X
C:\MyPrograms>c++ ifelse.cpp -o ifelse.exe         ▲
C:\MyPrograms>ifelse
Number exceeds five                                ▼
```

### Beware

Avoid nesting more
than three levels of **if**
statements – to avoid
confusion and errors.

9   Edit the integer variable declaration to change its value
    **int num = 3 ;**

10  Save, compile, and run the program again to see both
    tests now fail – executing the outer **else** statement

```
Command Prompt                                    _ □ X
C:\MyPrograms>c++ ifelse.cpp -o ifelse.exe         ▲
C:\MyPrograms>ifelse
Number is five or less                             ▼
```

# Switching branches

The **if** and **else** keywords, introduced on the previous page, allow programs to branch in a particular direction according to the result of a test condition and can be used to repeatedly test a variable to match a value. For example, testing for an integer:

```
if ( num == 1 ) { cout << "Monday" ;   }
else
if ( num == 2 ) { cout << "Tuesday" ;   }
else
if ( num == 3 ) { cout << "Wednesday" ; }
else
if ( num == 4 ) { cout << "Thursday" ; }
else
if ( num == 5 ) { cout << "Friday" ;      }
```

The program will branch in the direction of the match.

Conditional branching with long **if-else** statements can often be more efficiently performed using a **switch** statement instead, especially when the test expression evaluates one variable.

The **switch** statement works in an unusual way. It takes a given variable value then seeks a matching value among a number of **case** statements. Statements associated with the matching case statement value will then be executed.

When no match is found, no **case** statements will be executed but you may add a **default** statement after the final **case** statement to specify statements to be executed when no match is found.

It is important to follow each case statement with the **break** keyword to stop the program proceeding through the switch block after all statements associated with the matched **case** value have been executed – unless that is precisely what you require. For example, one statement for each block of three values like this:

```
switch( variable-name )
{
  case value1 ; case value2 ; case value3 ;
        statements-to-be-executed ; break ;

case value4 ; case value5 ; case value6 ;
        statements-to-be-executed ; break ;
}
```

Usually each **case** statement will have its own set of statements to execute and be terminated by a **break** as in the program opposite.

46

① Start a new program by specifying the C++ library classes to include and a namespace prefix to use
```
#include <iostream>
using namespace std ;
```

switch.cpp

② Add a main function containing a final return statement
```
int main()
{
  // Program code goes here.
  return 0 ;
}
```

③ In the main function, insert a statement to declare and initialize an integer variable with a value to be matched
```
int num = 3 ;
```

④ Next insert a switch statement to seek a match
```
switch ( num )
{
  case 1 : cout << num << " : Monday" ;        break ;
  case 2 : cout << num << " : Tuesday" ;       break ;
  case 3 : cout << num << " : Wednesday" ;     break ;
  case 4 : cout << num << " : Thursday" ;      break ;
  case 5 : cout << num << " : Friday" ;        break ;
}
```

⑤ In the switch statement, insert a default statement after the final case statement
```
default : cout << num << " : Weekend day" ;
```

⑥ Save, compile, and run the program to see the output

⑦ Now edit the integer variable declaration to change its value then save, compile and run the program once more
```
int num = 6 ;
```

47

Hot tip

Notice that a **default** statement does not need to be followed by a **break** keyword – because a **default** statement always appears last in a **switch** statement.

```
Command Prompt                                          _ □ ×
C:\MyPrograms>c++ switch.cpp -o switch.exe
C:\MyPrograms>switch
3 : Wednesday

C:\MyPrograms>c++ switch.cpp -o switch.exe
C:\MyPrograms>switch
6 : Weekend day
```

# Looping for

A loop is a piece of code in a program that automatically repeats. One complete execution of all statements contained within the loop block is known as an "iteration" or "pass".

The number of iterations made by a loop is controlled by a conditional test made within the loop. While the tested expression remains **true** the loop will continue – until the tested expression becomes **false**, at which time the loop ends.

The three types of loop structures in C++ programming are **for** loops, **while** loops, and **do-while** loops. Perhaps the most commonly used loop is the **for** loop, which has this syntax:

**for (** *initializer* **;** *test-expression* **;** *incrementer* **) {** *statements* **}**

The initializer sets the starting value for a counter of the number of iterations made by the loop. An integer variable is used for this purpose and is traditionally named "i".

Upon each iteration of the loop the test expression is evaluated and that iteration will only continue while this expression is **true**. When the tested expression becomes **false** the loop ends immediately without executing the statements again. On each iteration the counter is incremented then the statements executed.

Loops may be nested within other loops – so that the inner loop will fully execute its iterations on each iteration of the outer loop.

forloop.cpp

1   Start a new program by specifying the C++ library classes to include and a namespace prefix to use
```
#include <iostream>
using namespace std ;
```

2   Add a main function containing a final return statement
```
int main()
{
  // Program code goes here.
  return 0 ;
}
```

3   In the main function, insert a statement to declare an integer variable to be used as a loop iteration counter
```
int i ;
```

**4**  Next insert a for loop to output the counter value on each of three iterations

```
for ( i = 1 ; i < 4 ; i++ )
{
  cout << "Loop iteration: " << i << endl ;
}
```

**5**  Save, compile, and run the program to see the output

```
Command Prompt                                    _ □ ×

C:\MyPrograms>c++ forloop.cpp -o forloop.exe

C:\MyPrograms>forloop
Loop iteration: 1
Loop iteration: 2
Loop iteration: 3

C:\MyPrograms>_
```

**6**  Now edit the variable declaration to add a second counter

```
int i , j ;              // Integer variable "j" added.
```

**7**  Inside the for loop block, after the output statement add an inner loop to output its counter value on each iteration

```
for ( j = 1 ; j < 4 ; j++ )
{ cout << "   Inner loop iteration: " << j << endl ;      }
```

**8**  Save, compile, and run the program again to see the inner loop fully execute on each iteration of the outer loop

```
Command Prompt                                    _ □ ×

C:\MyPrograms>c++ forloop.cpp -o forloop.exe

C:\MyPrograms>forloop
Loop iteration: 1
     Inner loop iteration: 1
     Inner loop iteration: 2
     Inner loop iteration: 3
Loop iteration: 2
     Inner loop iteration: 1
     Inner loop iteration: 2
     Inner loop iteration: 3
Loop iteration: 3
     Inner loop iteration: 1
     Inner loop iteration: 2
     Inner loop iteration: 3

C:\MyPrograms>_
```

**Hot tip**

Alternatively, a for loop counter can count down by decrementing the counter value on each iteration using i-- instead of the i++ incrementer.

49

**Don't forget**

On the third iteration of these loops the incrementer increases the counter value to four – so when it is next evaluated the test returns false and the loop ends.

# Looping while

An alternative to the **for** loop, introduced on the previous page, uses the **while** keyword followed by an expression to be evaluated. When the expression is **true** statements contained within braces following the test expression will be executed. The expression will then be evaluated again and the **while** loop will continue until the expression is found to be **false**.

The loop's statement block <u>must</u> contain code that will affect the tested expression in order to change the evaluation result to **false**, otherwise an infinite loop is created that will lock the system! When the tested expression is found to be false upon its first evaluation, the while loop's statement block will never be executed.

A subtle variation of the while loop places the **do** keyword before the loop's statement block and a **while** test after it, with this syntax:

**do { statements-to-be-executed } while ( test-expression ) ;**

In a **do-while** loop the statement block will always be executed at least once – because the expression is not evaluated until after the first iteration of the loop.

A **break** statement can be included in any kind of loop to immediately terminate the loop when a test condition is met. The **break** ensures no further iterations of that loop will be executed.

Similarly a **continue** statement can be included in any kind of loop to immediately terminate that particular iteration of the loop when a test condition is met. The **continue** allows the loop to proceed to the next iteration.

### Hot tip

If you accidentally start running an infinite loop press the **Ctrl+C** keys to terminate the process.

50

while.cpp

1 Start a new program by specifying the C++ library classes to include and a namespace prefix to use
```
#include <vector>              // Include vector support.
#include <iostream>
using namespace std ;
```

2 Add a main function containing a final return statement
```
int main()
{
  // Program code goes here.
  return 0 ;
}
```

**3** In the main function, insert statements to declare an integer vector and an integer variable loop counter

```
vector <int> vec( 10 ) ;
int i = 0 ;
```

**4** Next insert a while loop to assign a counter value to an element of the vector on each iteration

```
while( i < vec.size() )
{
  i++ ;                          // Increment the counter.
  vec[ i-1 ] = i ;               // Assign count to element.
  cout << " | " << vec.at( i-1 ) ;
}
```

**Don't forget**

The vector library must be included with a preprocessor directive in this example.

**5** Save compile and run the program to see the output

```
Command Prompt                                    _ □ ×

C:\MyPrograms>c++ while.cpp -o while.exe

C:\MyPrograms>while
 | 1 | 2 | 3 | 4 | 5 | 6 | 7 | 8 | 9 | 10

C:\MyPrograms>_
```

**6** Edit the **while** loop to add a **continue** statement immediately after the incrementer to make the loop skip its third iteration

```
if ( i == 3 ) { cout << " | Skipped" ; continue ; }
```

**7** After the **continue** statement, now add a **break** statement, to make the loop quit on its eighth iteration

```
if ( i == 8 ) { cout << endl << "Done" ; break ;        }
```

**Beware**

The position of break and continue statements is important – they must appear after the incrementer, to avoid creating an infinite loop, but before other statements that affect the program to avoid executing those statements.

**8** Save, compile, and run the program once more to see the loop now omits some iterations

```
Command Prompt                                    _ □ ×

C:\MyPrograms>c++ while.cpp -o while.exe

C:\MyPrograms>while
 | 1 | 2 | Skipped | 4 | 5 | 6 | 7
Done

C:\MyPrograms>_
```

# Declaring functions

Functions enclose a section of code that provides specific functionality to the program. When a function is called from the main program its statements are executed and, optionally, a value can be returned to the main program upon completion. There are three main benefits to using functions:

- Functions make program code easier to understand & maintain
- Tried and tested functions can be re-used by other programs
- Several programmers can divide the workload in large projects by working on different functions of the program

## Declaring functions

Each function is declared early in the program code as a "prototype" comprising a data type for the value it will return and the function name followed by parentheses, which may optionally contain a list of "argument" data types of passed values it may use. The syntax of a function prototype declaration looks like this:

*return-data-type function-name ( arguments-data-type-list ) ;*

For example, a function named "computeArea" that returns a float value and is passed two float arguments is declared as:

**float computeArea( float, float ) ;**

## Defining functions

The function's definition appears later in the program code and comprises a repeat of the prototype plus the actual function body. The function body is the statements to be executed whenever the function is called, contained within a pair of braces.

It is important to recognize that the compiler checks the function definition against the prototype so the actual returned data type must match that specified in the prototype, and any supplied arguments must match in both number and data type. Compilation fails if the definition does not match the prototype. A simple **computeArea** definition might look like this:

```
float computeArea( float width, float height )
{
        return ( width * height ) ;
}
```

**Hot tip**

Strictly speaking, the arguments in a function prototype are known as its "formal parameters".

**Don't forget**

Use the **void** keyword if the function will return no value to the caller.

## Variable scope

Variables that are declared in a function can only be used locally within that function and are not accessible globally for use in other functions. This limitation is known as "variable scope".

1 Start a new program by specifying the C++ library classes to include and a namespace prefix to use
```
#include <iostream>
using namespace std ;
```

scope.cpp

2 Next declare two simple function prototypes
```
float bodyTempC() ;
float bodyTempF() ;
```

3 Now add a main function containing calls to each function and a final return statement
```
int main()
{
  cout << "Centigrade: " << bodyTempC() << endl ;
  cout << "Fahrenheit: " << bodyTempF() << endl ;
  return 0 ;
}
```

4 After the main function, define both other functions – to each return the value of a local "temperature" variable
```
float bodyTempC()
{
  float temperature = 37.0 ;
  return temperature ;
}

float bodyTempF()
{
  float temperature = 98.6 ;
  return temperature ;
}
```

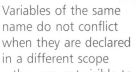

Hot tip

Variables of the same name do not conflict when they are declared in a different scope – they are not visible to each other.

53

5 Save, compile, and run the program to see the output

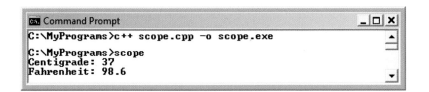

```
Command Prompt                                    _ □ ×
C:\MyPrograms>c++ scope.cpp -o scope.exe
C:\MyPrograms>scope
Centigrade: 37
Fahrenheit: 98.6
```

# Passing function arguments

Function calls frequently supply argument values to a function. These can be of any quantity and data type but they must agree with those specified in the function prototype declaration.

Note that arguments passed to a function only supply a copy of the original value, in a procedure known as "passing by value".

The values passed to arguments can be "static" values, specified in the program code, or "dynamic" values that are input by the user. At a command prompt the C++ **cin** function can be used with the **>>** input stream operator to direct a value from standard input to a variable like this:

```
float num ;
cout << "Please enter a number: " ;
cin >> num ;
```

Input can then be passed to a function as an argument in a function call, such as **workWith( num )**.

Optionally, a function prototype can assign default values to arguments, which will be used when a call does not pass an argument value. Multiple arguments can be assigned default values in the prototype but these must always appear at the end of the argument list, after any other arguments.

In the same way that functions can be called from the main function, functions may call other functions and pass arguments.

54

args.cpp

1   Start a new program by specifying the C++ library classes to include and a namespace prefix to use
```
#include <iostream>
using namespace std ;
```

2   Next declare a function prototype that returns a float value and specifies a single float argument, to which a default value is assigned
```
float fToC ( float degreesF= 32.0 ) ;
```

3   Add a main function containing a final return statement
```
int main()
{
  // Program code goes here.
  return 0 ;
}
```

**4** After the main function, define the "fToC" function with statements that will return a converted value

```
float fToC( float degreesF )
{
  float degreesC = ( (5.0 / 9.0 ) * ( degreesF - 32.0 ) ) ;
  return degreesC ;
}
```

**5** In the main function, insert a statement to declare two **float** variables – to store an input Fahrenheit temperature value and its Centigrade equivalent

```
float fahrenheit, centigrade ;
```

**6** Insert statements to request that user input be stored in the first variable

```
cout << "Enter a Fahrenheit temperature:\t" ;
cin >> fahrenheit ;
```

**7** Next call the "fToC" function to convert the input value – and assign the conversion to the second variable

```
centigrade = fToC( fahrenheit ) ;
```

**8** Now output a message describing the result

```
cout << fahrenheit << "F is " << centigrade << "C" ;
```

**9** Finally add a statement to output a further message using the default argument value of the function prototype

```
cout << endl << "Freezing point: " << fToC() << "C" ;
```

**10** Save, compile, and run the program, then enter a numeric value when requested to see the output

### Hot tip

In the same way that functions can be called from the main function, functions may call other functions and pass arguments to them.

### Don't forget

The names given to the arguments and variables in the function definition do not need to be the same as the variable names in the calling function – but it helps to clarify the program.

```
Command Prompt                                    _ □ ×

C:\MyPrograms>c++ args.cpp -o args.exe

C:\MyPrograms>args
Enter a Fahrenheit temperature: 98.6
98.6F is 37C
Freezing point: 0C

C:\MyPrograms>args
Enter a Fahrenheit temperature: 50
50F is 10C
Freezing point: 0C
```

# Overloading functions

Function "overloading" allows functions of the same name to happily co-exist in the same program, providing their arguments differ in number, data type, or both number and data type. The compiler matches a function call to the correct version of the function by recognizing its argument number and data types – a process known as "function resolution".

It is useful to create overloaded functions when the tasks they are to perform are similar, yet subtly different.

overload.cpp

**1** Start a new program by specifying the C++ library classes to include and a namespace prefix to use
```
#include <iostream>
using namespace std ;
```

**2** Below the preprocessor instructions, declare a function prototype that returns a float value and has one argument
```
float computeArea( float ) ;
```

**3** Now declare two overloaded function prototypes – having different arguments to the first prototype
```
float computeArea( float, float ) ;
float computeArea( char, float, float ) ;
```

**4** Below the prototype declarations, add a main function containing a final return statement
```
int main()
{
   // Program code goes here.
   return 0 ;
}
```

**5** After the main function, define the first function that receives just one argument
```
float computeArea( float diameter )
{
   float radius = ( diameter / 2 ) ;
   return ( 3.141593 * ( radius * radius ) ) ;
}
```

56

**6** Below the first function definition, define the overloaded functions that receives different arguments

```
float computeArea( float width, float height )
{
  return ( width * height) ;
}

float computeArea( char letter, float width , float height )
{
  return ( ( width / 2 ) * height ) ;
}
```

**7** In the main function, insert statements to declare two variables and initialize one with user input

```
float num, area ;

cout << "Enter dimension in feet: " ;
cin >> num ;
```

**8** Call the first function and output its returned value

```
area = computeArea( num ) ;
cout << "Circle: Area = " << area << " sq.ft." << endl ;
```

**9** Call the overloaded functions and output their returns

```
area = computeArea( num, num ) ;
cout << "Square: Area = "<< area << " sq.ft." << endl ;
area = computeArea( 'T', num, num ) ;
cout << "Triangle: Area = "<< area << "sq.ft." << endl ;
```

**10** Save, compile, and run the program then enter a numeric value when requested to see the output

```
C:\MyPrograms>c++ overload.cpp -o overload.exe

C:\MyPrograms>overload
Enter dimension in feet: 4
Circle: Area = 12.5664 sq.ft.
Square: Area = 16 sq.ft.
Triangle: Area = 8sq.ft.

C:\MyPrograms>overload
Enter dimension in feet: 2.5
Circle: Area = 4.90874 sq.ft.
Square: Area = 6.25 sq.ft.
Triangle: Area = 3.125sq.ft.
```

**Don't forget**

The value passed to the **char** argument is never used – that argument is included merely to differentiate that overloaded function.

# Optimizing functions

Functions can call themselves recursively, to repeatedly execute the statements contained in their function body – much like a loop. As with loops, a recursive function must contain an incrementer and a conditional test to call itself again or stop repeating when a condition is met. The syntax of a recursive function looks like this:

*return-data-type function-name* ( *argument-list* )
{
      *statements-to-be-executed* ;
      *incrementer* ;
      *conditional-test-to-recall-or-exit* ;
}

The incrementer will change the value of a passed argument – so subsequent calls will pass the adjusted value back to the function.

optimize.cpp

1. Start a new program by specifying the C++ library classes to include and a namespace prefix to use
```
#include <iostream>
using namespace std ;
```

2. Below the preprocessor instructions, declare two function prototypes that will both be recursive functions
```
int computeFactorials( int, int ) ;
int factorial( int ) ;
```

3. Below the prototype declarations, add a main function containing a final return statement
```
int main()
{
  // Program code goes here.
  return 0 ;
}
```

### Hot tip

A recursive function generally uses more system resources than a loop – but it can make for more readable code.

4. After the main function, add the definition for the first function prototype – a recursive function
```
int computeFactorials( int num, int max )
{
  cout << "Factorial of " << num << ": ";
  cout << factorial( num ) << endl ;      // Statements.
  num++ ;                                  // Incrementer.
  if( num > max ) return 0 ;               // Exit...
  else computeFactorials( num , max ) ;    // or recall.
}
```

**5** Define a recursive function for the second prototype

```
int factorial( int n )
{
  int result ;
  if( n == 1 ) result = 1 ;            // Exit or...
  else result = ( factorial( n - 1 ) * n );    // Decrement..
  return result ;                      // and recall.
}
```

**6** At the start of the main function, insert a call to the recursive function

```
computeFactorials( 1, 8 ) ;
```

**7** Save, compile, and run the program to see the output

```
Command Prompt                                    _ □ ×

C:\MyPrograms>c++ optimize.cpp -o optimize.exe

C:\MyPrograms>optimize
Factorial of 1: 1
Factorial of 2: 2
Factorial of 3: 6
Factorial of 4: 24
Factorial of 5: 120
Factorial of 6: 720
Factorial of 7: 5040
Factorial of 8: 40320

C:\MyPrograms>_
```

The output lists factorial values (factorial 3 is 3x2x1=6, etc.) but the program can be improved by optimizing the **factorial()** function. This function does not need a variable if written with the ternary operator. It then contains just one statement so its definition can replace the prototype declaration as an "inline" declaration. This means that the program need not keep checking between the declaration and definition, and so improves efficiency.

**8** Delete the **factorial()** function definition, then replace its prototype declaration with this inline declaration

```
inline int factorial( int n )
{ return ( n == 1 ) ? 1 : ( factorial( n - 1 ) * n ); }
```

**9** Save, compile, and run the program again to see the same output, produced more efficiently

**Don't forget**

If you accidentally run an infinite recursive function press the **Ctrl+C** keys to terminate the process.

**Beware**

Inline declarations may only contain one or two statements as the compiler recreates them at each calling point – longer inline declarations would, therefore, produce a more unwieldy program.

# Summary

- An **if** statement evaluates a given test expression for a boolean value of **true** or **false**

- Statements contained in braces after an **if** statement will only be executed when the evaluation is found to be **true**

- The **if** and **else** keywords are used to perform conditional branching according to the result of a tested expression

- A **switch** statement is an alternative form of conditional branching that matches a **case** statement to a given value

- The **for** loop structure has parameters declaring an initializer, a test expression, and an incrementer or decrementer

- A **while** loop and **do-while** loop must always have an incrementer or decrementer within their loop body

- Any type of loop can be immediately terminated by including a **break** statement within the loop body

- A single iteration of any type of loop can be skipped by including a **continue** statement within the loop body

- Functions are usually declared as prototypes at the start of the program and defined after the main function

- Variables declared in a function are only accessible from within that function as they only have local scope

- Values can be passed into functions if arguments are declared in the function prototype and definition

- Overloaded functions have the same name but different number or type of declared arguments

- Recursive functions repeatedly call themselves until a test condition is met

- Short function definitions of just one or two statements can be declared in place of a prototype using the **inline** keyword

# 4 Handling strings

*This chapter demonstrates how to manipulate C++ text strings as a simpler, more powerful alternative to character arrays.*

# Creating string variables

Unlike the **char, int, float, double,** and **bool** data types there is no native "string" data type in C++ – but its **<string>** library class provides a **string** object that emulates a string data type. To make this available to a program the library must be added with an **#include <string>** directive at the start of the program.

Like the **<iostream>** class library, the **<string>** library is part of the **std** namespace that is used by the C++ standard library classes. This means that a string object can be referred to as **std::string,** or more simply as **string** when a **using namespace std;** directive is included at the start of the program.

Once the **<string>** library is made available a **string** "variable" can be declared in the same way as other variables. The declaration may optionally initialize the variable using the = assignment operator, or it may be initialized later in the program.

Additionally, a **string** variable may be initialized by including a text string between parentheses after the variable name.

Text strings in C++ must always be enclosed within " " double quote characters – ' ' single quotes are only used to surround character values of the **char** data type.

A C++ **string** variable is much easier to work with than the **char** arrays which C programmers must use, as it automatically resizes to accommodate the length of any text string. At a lower level the text is still stored as a character array but the **string** variable lets you ignore those details. Consequently a character array can be assigned to a **string** variable using the = assignment operator.

It is important to remember that when numeric values are assigned to a **string** variable they are no longer a numeric data type, so arithmetic cannot be performed on them. For example, attempting to add **string** values of "7" and "6" with the + addition operator produces the concatenated **string** "76", not the numerical value of 13. In this case the + operator recognizes that the context is not arithmetical so adopts the guise of "concatenation operator" to unite the two strings. Similarly, the **+=** operator appends a **string** to another **string** and is useful to build long strings of text.

Several **string** values are built into a single long string in the example program described on the opposite page.

1. Start a new program by specifying the C++ library classes to include and a namespace prefix to use

```
#include <string>          // Include string support.
#include <iostream>
using namespace std ;
```

string.cpp

2. Add a main function containing four string variable declarations and a final return statement

```
int main()
{
  string text = "9" ;
  string term( "9 " ) ;
  string info = "Toys" ;
  string color ;
  // Add more statements here.
  return 0 ;
}
```

3. In the main function, after the variable declarations insert statements to declare and initialize a character array, then assign its value to the uninitialized string variable

```
char hue[4] = { 'R', 'e', 'd', '\0' } ;
color = hue ;
```

4. Assign a longer text string to one of the string variables

```
info = "Balloons" ;
```

5. Build a long string by combining all the string variable values in the first string variable, then output the combined string value

```
text += ( term + color + info ) ;
cout << endl << text << endl ;
```

Don't forget

Remember to add the special **\0** character to mark the end of a string in a **char** array.

6. Save, compile, and run the program to see the output

```
Command Prompt                                    _ □ X

C:\MyPrograms>c++ string.cpp -o string.exe

C:\MyPrograms>string

99 Red Balloons

C:\MyPrograms>_
```

63

# Getting string input

The C++ **cin** function, that was introduced in the last chapter to input numeric values, can also assign text input to **string** variables. This has a limitation as it can only be used to input a single word at a time – the **cin** function stops reading the input when it encounters a space, leaving any other text in the "input buffer".

When you want to allow the user to input a string with spaces, such as a sentence, the **getline()** function can be used. This function requires two arguments to specify the source and destination of the string. For example, where the **cin** function is the source and a string variable named "str" is the destination:

**getline( cin , str ) ;**

The **getline()** function reads from an input "stream" until it encounters a **\n** newline character at the end of the line – created when you hit Return.

Care must be taken when mixing **cin** and **getline()** functions as the **getline()** function will automatically read anything left on the input buffer – giving the impression that the program is skipping an instruction. The **cin.ignore()** function can be used to overcome this problem by ignoring content left in the input buffer.

input.cpp

① Start a new program by specifying the C++ library classes to include and a namespace prefix to use
```
#include <string>              // Include string support.
#include <iostream>
using namespace std ;
```

② Add a main function containing one string variable declaration and a final return statement
```
int main()
{
  string name ;
  // Add more statements here.
  return 0 ;
}
```

③ In the main function, insert statements assigning the user name input to a string variable then outputting its value
```
cout << "Please enter your full name: " ;
cin >> name ;
cout << "Welcome " << name << endl ;
```

**4** Next insert a statement requesting the user name again, but this time assigning the input to the string variable with the getline function before outputting its value
```
cout << "Please re-enter your full name: " ;
getline( cin , name ) ;
cout << "Thanks, " << name << endl ;
```

**5** Save, compile, and run the program and enter your full name when requested

```
Command Prompt                                    _ □ X
C:\MyPrograms>c++ input.cpp -o input.exe

C:\MyPrograms>input
Please enter your full name: Mike McGrath
Welcome Mike
Please re-enter your full name: Thanks,  McGrath

C:\MyPrograms>_
```

This unsatisfactory result shows that **cin** reads up to the first space, leaving the second name in the input buffer, which is then read by **getline()** and subsequently output. The problem persists even when you enter only your first name because **cin** leaves the newline character, created when you hit Return, on the input buffer.

**6** Edit the program to resolve this issue by inserting a statement, just before the call to the getline function, instructing it to ignore content in the input buffer
```
cin.ignore( 256, '\n' ) ;
```

**7** Save, compile, and run the program again then re-enter your full name to see the program perform as required

```
Command Prompt                                    _ □ X
C:\MyPrograms>c++ input.cpp -o input.exe

C:\MyPrograms>input
Please enter your full name: Mike McGrath
Welcome Mike
Please re-enter your full name: Mike McGrath
Thanks, Mike McGrath

C:\MyPrograms>_
```

**Don't forget**

Use the **cin** function for numeric input or single word input, but use the **getline()** function for string input.

**Hot tip**

The arguments to the **cin.ignore()** function specify it should discard up to 256 characters and stop when it encounters a newline character.

65

# Solving the string problem

A problem arises with **string** variables when you need to convert them to a different data type, perhaps to perform arithmetical operations with those values. As the **string** object is not a native C++ data type a **string** variable value cannot be converted to an **int** or any other regular data type by casting.

The solution is provided by the C++ **<sstream>** library that allows a **stringstream** object to act as an intermediary, through which **string** values can be converted to a numeric data type, and numeric values can be converted to a **string** data type. To make this ability available to a program the library must be added with an **#include <sstream>** directive at the start of the program.

Values can be loaded into a **stringstream** object with the familiar output stream **<<** operator – that is used with **cout** statements. Contents can then be extracted from a **stringstream** object with the **>>** input stream operator that is used with **cin** statements.

In order to re-use a **stringstream** object it must first be returned to its original state. This requires its contents to be set as an empty **string** and it status bit flags to be cleared.

convert.cpp

1. Start a new program by specifying the C++ library classes to include and a namespace prefix to use

```
#include <string>        // Include string support.
#include <sstream>       // Include stringstream support.
#include <iostream>
using namespace std ;
```

2. Add a main function containing a final return statement and declaring two initialized variables to be converted

```
int main()
{
  string term = "100" ;
  int number = 100 ;
  // Add more statements here.
  return 0 ;
}
```

3. In the main function, insert statements to declare an integer variable, string variable, and a stringstream object

```
int num ;                    // To store a converted string.
string text ;                // To store a converted integer.
stringstream stream ;        // To perform conversions.
```

**4** Next use the stream output operator to load the initialized string value into the stringstream object

```
stream << term ;        // Load the string.
```

**5** Use the stream input operator to extract content from the stringstream object into the uninitialized integer variable

```
stream >> num ;         // Extract the integer.
```

**6** Perform arithmetic on the integer and output the result

```
num /= 4 ;
cout << "Integer value: " << num << endl ;
```

**7** Reset the stringstream object ready for re-use

```
stream.str("") ;        // Empty the contents.
stream.clear() ;        // Empty the bit flags.
```

**8** Now use the stream output operator to load the initialized integer value into the stringstream object

```
stream << number ;      // Load the integer.
```

**9** Use the stream input operator to extract content from the stringstream object into the uninitialized string variable

```
stream >> text ;        // Extract the string.
```

**10** Perform concatenation on the string and output the result

```
text += " Per Cent" ;
cout << "String value: " << text << endl ;
```

**11** Save, compile, and run the program to see the converted output values

```
Command Prompt                                          _ □ X

C:\MyPrograms>c++ convert.cpp -o convert.exe

C:\MyPrograms>convert
Integer value:   25
String value:    100 Per Cent

C:\MyPrograms>_
```

**Hot tip**

Notice how the **stringstream** object's **str()** function is used here to reset its contents to an empty string.

67

**Don't forget**

A non-empty **stringstream** object has bit flags indicating its status as **good**, **bad**, **eof**, or **fail** – these should be cleared before re-use by the **stringstream** object's **clear()** function, as demonstrated here.

# Discovering string features

The C++ **<string>** library provides a number of functions that make it easy to work with strings. To use them simply add the function name after the **string** variable name and a dot. For example, with a **string** variable named "msg" you can call upon the **size()** function, to return its character length, with **msg.size()**.

A **string** variable can be emptied of all characters by assigning it an empty string with two double quotes without spacing – as "", or alternatively by calling the **<string>** library's **clear()** function.

Unlike a **char** array a **string** variable will dynamically enlarge to accommodate the number of characters assigned to it, and its current memory size can be revealed with the **<string>** library's **capacity()** function. Once enlarged the allocated memory size remains, even when a smaller **string** gets assigned to the variable.

The **<string>** library's **empty()** function returns a boolean **true** (1) or **false** (0) response to reveal whether the string is empty or not.

**Hot tip**

The **length()** function can be used in place of the **size()** function to reveal the size of a string value.

features.cpp

1.  Start a new program by specifying the C++ library classes to include and a namespace prefix to use
    ```
    #include <string>          // Include string support.
    #include <iostream>
    using namespace std ;
    ```

2.  Below the preprocessor directives, declare a function prototype with a single string data type argument
    ```
    void computeFeatures( string ) ;
    ```

3.  Add a main function containing a final return statement and declaring an initialized string variable
    ```
    int main()
    {
      string text = "C++ is fun" ;
      // Add more statements here.
      return 0 ;
    }
    ```

4.  After the main function, define the declared function to display the string variable value when called
    ```
    void computeFeatures( string text )
    {
      cout << endl << "String: " << text << endl ;
    }
    ```

**5** In the function definition, add statements to output features of the string variable
```
cout << "Size:   " << text.size() ;
cout << "    Capacity: " << text.capacity() ;
cout << "    Empty?: " << text.empty() << endl ;
```

**6** In the main function, insert a call to the defined function
```
computeFeatures( text ) ;
```

**7** Next in the main function, insert a statement to enlarge the string value and call the function to see its features
```
text += " for everyone" ;
computeFeatures( text ) ;
```

**8** Now insert a statement to reduce the string value
```
text = "C++ Fun" ;
computeFeatures( text ) ;
```

**9** Finally insert a statement to empty the string variable
```
text.clear() ;
computeFeatures( text ) ;
```

**10** Save, compile, and run the program to see the output

```
Command Prompt                                    _ □ ×

C:\MyPrograms>c++ features.cpp -o features.exe

C:\MyPrograms>features

String: C++ is fun
Size:  10        Capacity: 10     Empty?: 0

String: C++ is fun for everyone
Size:  23        Capacity: 23     Empty?: 0

String: C++ Fun
Size:  7         Capacity: 23     Empty?: 0

String:
Size:  0         Capacity: 23     Empty?: 1

C:\MyPrograms>_
```

**Hot tip**

The **empty()** function is useful to check if the user has entered requested input.

**Don't forget**

A space occupies one memory element – just like a character does.

# Joining & comparing strings

When the **+** operator is used to concatenate strings in an assignment the combined strings get stored in the **string** variable. But when it is used with the **cout** function the strings are only combined in the output – the variable values are unchanged.

The **<string>** library's **append()** function can also be used to concatenate strings, specifying the **string** value to append as an argument within its parentheses. When this is used with the **cout** function the strings are combined in the variable, then its value written as output – in this case the variable value does change.

String comparisons can be made, in the same way as numeric comparisons, with the **==** equality operator. This returns **true** (1) when both strings precisely match, otherwise it returns **false** (0).

Alternatively, the **<string>** library's **compare()** function can be used to compare a **string** value specified as its argument. Unlike the **==** equality comparison, the **compare()** function returns zero when the strings are identical by examining the **string** value's combined ASCII code values. When the **string** argument totals more than the first string it returns -1, otherwise it returns 1.

compare.cpp

1. Start a new program by specifying the C++ library classes to include and a namespace prefix to use
```
#include <string>            // Include string support.
#include <iostream>
using namespace std ;
```

2. Add a main function containing a final return statement and declaring three initialized string variables
```
int main()
{
  string lang = "C++" ;
  string term = " Programming" ;
  string text = "C++ Programming" ;
  // Add more statements here.
  return 0 ;
}
```

70

**3** In the main function, insert statements to output two string values combined with the + concatenate operator and the (unchanged) value of the first variable

```
cout << "Concatenated: " << ( lang + term ) << endl ;
cout << "Original: " << lang << endl ;
```

**Don't forget**

The += assignment operator can also be used to append a string.

**4** Next insert statements to output two string values combined with the append function and the (changed) value of the first variable

```
cout << "Appended: " << lang.append( term ) << endl;
cout << "Original: " << lang << endl << endl ;
```

**5** Use the == equality operator to compare two string values that differ, then two string values that match

```
cout << "Differ: " << ( lang == term ) << endl ;
cout << "Match: " << ( lang == text ) << endl << endl ;
```

**6** Now use the compare function to compare three string values, examining their ASCII code total values

```
cout << "Match: " << lang.compare( text ) << endl ;
cout << "Differ: " << lang.compare( term ) << endl ;
cout << "Lower ASCII: " <<
                lang.compare( "zzzzz" ) << endl ;
```

**7** Save, compile, and run the program to see the output

```
C:\MyPrograms>c++ compare.cpp -o compare.exe

C:\MyPrograms>compare
Concatenated: C++ Programming
Original: C++
Appended: C++ Programming
Original: C++ Programming

Differ: 0
Match: 1

Match: 0
Differ: 1
Lower ASCII: -1

C:\MyPrograms>_
```

**Hot tip**

In comparisons character order is taken into account – so comparing "za" to "az" reveals that "za" has a greater total. In terms of ASCII values 'a' is 97, and 'z' is 122.

71

# Copying & swapping strings

String values can be assigned to a **string** variable by the = assignment operator, or by the **<string>** library's **assign()** function. This function specifies the **string** value to be copied to the variable as an argument within its parentheses.

Optionally, the **assign()** function can copy just a part of the specified **string** value by stating the position of the starting character as a second argument, and the number of characters to copy as a third argument.

The contents of a **string** variable can be exchanged for that of another **string** variable by the **<string>** library's **swap()** function. In this case the contents of the first variable receives those of the second variable, which in turn receives those of the first variable.

swap.cpp

1  Start a new program by specifying the C++ library classes to include and a namespace prefix to use
```
#include <string>              // Include string support.
#include <iostream>
using namespace std ;
```

2  Add a main function containing a final return statement and declaring three string variables – with one initialized
```
int main()
{
  string front ;
  string back ;
  string text =
    "Always laugh when you can. It\'s cheap medicine." ;
  // Add more statements here.
  return 0 ;
}
```

3  In the main function, insert a statement to assign the entire value of the initialized string variable to the first uninitialized string variable
```
front.assign( text ) ;
```

4  Next insert a statement to output the newly assigned string value
```
cout << endl << "Front: " << front << endl ;
```

**5** Now insert a statement to assign only the first 27 characters of the initialized variable to the first variable
**front.assign( text, 0, 27 ) ;**

**6** Output the newly assigned string value
**cout << endl << "Front: " << front << endl ;**

**7** Next assign only the last part of the initialized string variable to the second uninitialized variable, starting at character (element) 27
**back.assign ( text, 27 , text.size() ) ;**

**8** Now output this newly assigned string value
**cout << "Back: " << back << endl ;**

**9** Finally exchange the assigned string values contained in the first and second string variables then output the exchanged values
**back.swap( front ) ;**
**cout << endl << "Front: " << front << endl ;**
**cout << "Back: " << back << endl ;**

**10** Save, compile, and run the program to see the output

### Hot tip

Use the = assignment operator to assign complete strings and the **assign()** function to assign partial strings.

```
Command Prompt                                           _ □ X

C:\MyPrograms>c++ swap.cpp -o swap.exe

C:\MyPrograms>swap

Front: Always laugh when you can. It's cheap medicine.

Front: Always laugh when you can.
Back: It's cheap medicine.

Front: It's cheap medicine.
Back: Always laugh when you can.

C:\MyPrograms>_
```

### Hot tip

Use the **swap()** function wherever possible rather than creating additional string variables.

# Finding substrings

A **string** value can be searched to see if it contains a specified "substring" using the **find()** function of the **<string>** library. Its parentheses should specify the substring to seek as its first argument, and the index number of the character at which to start searching as its second argument.

When a search successfully locates the specified substring the **find()** function returns the index number of the first occurrence of the substring's first character within the searched string. When the search fails **find()** returns a value of -1 to indicate failure.

There are several other functions in the **<string>** library that are related to the **find()** function. Two of these are the **find_first_of()** function and the **find_first_not_of()** function. Instead of seeking the first occurrence of a complete **string**, as **find()** does, the **find_first_of()** function seeks the first occurrence of any of the characters in a specified **string**, and **find_first_not_of()** seeks the first occurrence of a character that is not in the specified **string**.

The **find_last_of()** and **find_last_not_of()** functions work in a similar manner – but begin searching at the end of the **string** then move forwards.

find.cpp

**1** Start a new program by specifying the C++ library classes to include and a namespace prefix to use
```
#include <string>              // Include string support.
#include <iostream>
using namespace std ;
```

**2** Add a main function containing a final return statement, an initialized string variable declaration, and declaring an integer variable to store search results
```
int main()
{
  string text = "I can resist anything but temptation." ;
  int num ;
  // Add more statements here.
  return 0 ;
}
```

**3** In the main function, insert statements to output the start position of a substring within the entire string variable
```
num = text.find( "resist", 0 ) ;
cout << "Position: " << num << endl ;
```

**4** Next insert a statement to seek a non-existent substring within the entire string variable and output the result
```
num = text.find( "nonsuch" , 0 ) ;
cout << "Result:  " << num << endl ;
```

**5** Now insert a statement to output the start position of the first occurrence any characters of an "If" substring found within the entire string variable
```
num = text.find_first_of( "If" , 0 ) ;
cout << "First I: " << num << endl ;
```

Beware

**Beware**

The searches are case sensitive so seeking "If" and "if" may produce different results – here uppercase 'I' matches.

**6** Insert a statement to report the string position of the first character not within the "If" substring
```
num = text.find_first_not_of( "If" ) ;
cout << "First not I: " << num << endl ;
```

**7** Next insert a statement to seek the last occurrence of the letter "t" within the **string** variable and output its position
```
num = text.find_last_of( "t" ) ;
cout << "Last t: " << num << endl ;
```

**8** Now add a statement to report the string position of the last character within the **string** variable that is not a "t"
```
num = text.find_last_not_of( "t" ) ;
cout << "Last not t: " << num << endl ;
```

**9** Save, compile, and run the program to see the search results indicating failure or the positions when located

**Don't forget**

The first character in a string is at position zero, not at position one.

```
Command Prompt                                    _ □ ×

C:\MyPrograms>c++ find.cpp -o find.exe

C:\MyPrograms>find
Position: 6
Result: -1
First I: 0
First not I: 1
Last t: 32
Last not t: 36

C:\MyPrograms>_
```

75

# Replacing substrings

The **<string>** library contains a number of useful functions to manipulate substrings. A **string** can be inserted into another **string** using the **insert()** function. This requires the index position at which the **string** should be inserted as its first argument, and the **string** value to be inserted as its second argument.

Conversely, a substring can be removed from a **string** using the **erase()** function. This requires the index position at which it should begin erasing as its first argument, and the number of characters to be erased as its second argument.

The **replace()** function neatly combines the **erase()** and **insert()** functions to both remove a substring and insert a replacement. It requires three arguments specifying the position at which it should begin erasing, the number of characters to be erased, and the replacement **string** to be inserted at that position.

A substring can be copied from a **string** using the **substr()** function, stating the index position at which it should begin copying as its first argument, and the number of characters to be copied as its second argument.

The character at any specified position within a **string** can be copied using the **at()** function, which requires the index position as its argument. The final character in a **string** always has an element index number one less than the length of the **string** – because index numbering starts at zero, not one.

sub.cpp

1. Start a new program by specifying the C++ library classes to include and a namespace prefix to use
```
#include <string>          // Include string support.
#include <iostream>
using namespace std ;
```

2. Add a main function containing a final return statement, an initialized string variable declaration, and a statement outputting the string variable value
```
int main()
{
  string text = "I do like the seaside" ;
  cout << "Original: " << text << endl ;
  // Add more statements here.
  return 0 ;
}
```

**3** In the main function, insert statements to insert a substring into the variable value at index position ten and to output the modified string

**text.insert( 10, "to be beside " ) ;**
**cout << "Inserted: " << text << endl ;**

**4** Next insert statements to erase two characters from the modified string value starting at index position three, and to output the revised string

**text.erase( 2, 3 ) ;**
**cout << "Erased:  " << text << endl ;**

**5** Now insert statements to remove 25 characters at index position seven, insert a replacement substring, then output the revised string again

**text.replace( 7, 25, "strolling by the sea" ) ;**
**cout << "Replaced:  " << text << endl ;**

**6** Finally insert statements to output nine copied characters at index position seven, and to output the final character in the string

**cout << "Copied: " << text.substr( 7, 9 ) << endl ;**
**cout << "Last character: " <<**
                    **text.at( text.size() - 1 ) << endl ;**

**7** Save, compile, and run the program to see the output showing how the string has been manipulated

```
Command Prompt                                    _ □ ×

C:\MyPrograms>c++ sub.cpp -o sub.exe

C:\MyPrograms>sub
Original: I do like the seaside
Inserted: I do like to be beside the seaside
Erased:  I like to be beside the seaside
Replaced: I like strolling by the sea
Copied:   strolling
Last character: a

C:\MyPrograms>_
```

**Hot tip**

The **insert()** function can optionally have a third and fourth argument – specifying the position in the substring at which to begin copying, and the number of characters to be copied.

**Hot tip**

The **replace()** function can optionally have a fourth and fifth argument – specifying the position in the substring at which to begin copying, and the number of characters to be copied.

77

# Summary

- The C++ **<string>** library provides a "string" object that emulates a data type – so that **string** variables can be created

- Arithmetic cannot be performed on numeric values assigned to **string** variables until they are converted to a numeric data type

- The standard **cin** function reads from standard input until it encounters a space, so can be used to input a single word, and provides an **ignore()** function to disregard the input buffer

- The **getline()** function reads from standard input until it encounters a newline, so can be used to input a string of text

- The C++ **<sstream>** library provides a "stringstream" object that acts an intermediary to convert strings to other data types

- A **string** variable can be emptied by assigning it an empty string ( = "" ) or by calling its **clear()** function

- Features of a **string** variable can be revealed by calling its **size()**, **capacity()**, and **empty()** functions

- Multiple **string** values can be concatenated by the **+** operator

- A **string** can be appended to another **string** by the **+=** operator or by calling its **append()** function

- A **string** can be compared to another **string** by the **==** operator or by calling its **compare()** function

- A **string** value can be assigned to a **string** variable using the **=** operator or by calling its **assign()** function

- The **swap()** function swaps the values of two **string** variables

- Substrings of a **string** can be sought with the **find()** function, or specialized functions such as **find_first_of()** , and a character retrieved from a specified index position by the **at()** function

- A substring can be added to a **string** by its **insert()** function, removed by its **erase()** function, replaced by its **replace()** function, or copied by its **substr()** function

# 5

# Reading and writing files

*This chapter demonstrates how to store and retrieve data in text files, and illustrates how to avoid errors in C++ programs.*

# Writing a file

The ability to read and write files from a program provides a useful method of maintaining data on the computer's hard disk. The format of the data may be specified as human-readable plain text format or machine-readable binary format.

The standard C++ **<fstream>** library provides functions for working with files, which can be made available by adding an **#include <fstream>** directive at the start of the program.

For each file that is to be opened a filestream object must first be created. This will be either an "ofstream" (output filestream) object, for writing data to the file, or an "ifstream" (input filestream) object, for reading data from the file. The **ofstream** object is used like the **cout** function that writes to standard output, and the **ifstream** object works like the **cin** function that reads from standard input.

The declaration of a filestream object for writing output begins with the **ofstream** keyword, then a chosen name for that particular filestream object followed by parentheses nominating the text file to write to. So the declaration syntax looks like this:

**ofstream** *object-name* **(** *"file-name"* **) ;**

The argument nominating the text file may optionally contain the full file path, such as **"C:\data\log.txt"** or **"/home/user/log.txt"**, otherwise the program will seek the file within the directory in which the program resides.

Before writing output to a file the program should always first test that the filestream object has actually been created. Typically this is performed by an **if** statement that allows the program to write output only when the test is successful.

If a nominated file already exists it will, by default, be overwritten without warning. Otherwise a new file will be created and written.

After writing output to a nominated file the program should always call the associated filestream object's **close()** function to close the output filestream.

The program described opposite first builds a string for writing as output. This is written to a nominated file when the filestream object has been successfully created, then the filestream closed.

### Beware

The nominated file name or path must be enclosed within double quotes, like a **string**.

**1** Start a new program by specifying the C++ library classes to include and a namespace prefix to use

```
#include <fstream>      // Include filestream support.
#include <string>
#include <iostream>
using namespace std ;
```

write.cpp

**2** Add a main function containing a final return statement and building a lengthy text string in a string variable

```
int main()
{
  string poem = "\n\tI never saw a man who looked" ;
  poem.append( "\n\tWith such a wistful eye" ) ;
  poem.append( "\n\tUpon that little tent of blue" ) ;
  poem.append( "\n\tWhich prisoners call the sky" ) ;
  // Add more statements here.
  return 0 ;
}
```

Hot tip

String values can contain **\n** newline and **\t** tab escape sequences for formatting lines.

**3** In the main function, create an output filestream object

```
ofstream writer( "poem.txt" ) ;
```

**4** Insert statements to write the string to a file or exit, then save, compile, and run the program to see the result

```
if( ! writer )
{
  cout << "Error opening file for output" << endl ;
  return -1 ;    // Signal an error then exit the program.
}
writer << poem << endl ;      // Write output.
writer.close() ;              // Close filestream.
```

Don't forget

Notice how the newline and tab characters are preserved in the text file.

```
Command Prompt                                    _ □ ×
C:\MyPrograms>c++ write.cpp -o write.exe
C:\MyPrograms>write
```

```
poem.txt - Notepad                            □ □ ×
File  Edit  Format  View  Help
      I never saw a man who looked
      with such a wistful eye
      Upon that little tent of blue
      which prisoners call the sky
```

# Appending to a file

When a filestream object is created, the parentheses following its chosen name can optionally contain additional arguments, specifying a range of file "modes" to control the behavior of that filestream object. These file modes are part of the **ios** namespace, so must be explicitly addressed using that prefix. Each file mode is listed in the table below, together with a behavior description:

| Mode | Behavior |
| --- | --- |
| **ios::out** | open a file to write output |
| **ios::in** | open a file to read input |
| **ios::app** | open a file to append output at the end of any existing content |
| **ios::trunc** | truncate the existing file (default behavior) |
| **ios::ate** | open a file without truncating and allow data to be written anywhere in the file |
| **ios::binary** | treat the file as binary format rather than text so the data may be stored in non-text format |

Multiple modes may be specified if they are separated by a "|" pipe character. For example, the syntax of a statement to open a file for binary output looks like this:

**ofstream** *object-name* **( "***file-name***" , ios::out|ios::binary ) ;**

The default behavior when no modes are explicitly specified regards the file as a text file that will be truncated after writing.

The most commonly specified mode is **ios::app**, which ensures existing content will not be overwritten when new output is written to the nominated file.

The program described opposite appends data to the text file created in the previous example.

## Don't forget

The directive **using std;** allows the **std** namespace prefix to be omitted so **cout** refers to the **std::cout** function. The **ios** namespace exists within the **std** namespace – so the file modes can be explicitly addressed using both namespace prefixes, for example **std::ios::out**.

**1** Start a new program by specifying the C++ library classes to include and a namespace prefix to use

```cpp
#include <fstream>      // Include filestream support.
#include <string>
#include <iostream>
using namespace std ;
```

append.cpp

**2** Add a main function containing a final return statement and building a text string in a string variable

```cpp
int main()
{
  string info = "\n\tThe Ballad of Reading Gaol" ;
  info.append( "\n\t\t\tOscar Wilde 1898" ) ;
  // Add more statements here.
  return 0 ;
}
```

**3** In the main function, create an output filestream object – specifying a file mode that will append to existing text

```cpp
ofstream writer( "poem.txt" , ios::app ) ;
```

**4** Insert statements to append the string to a file or exit, then save, compile, and run the program to see the result

```cpp
if( ! writer )
{
  cout << "Error opening file for output" << endl ;
  return -1 ;     // Signal an error then exit the program.
}
writer << info << endl ;        // Append output.
writer.close() ;                // Close filestream.
```

**Beware**

The file must allow the program suitable read and write permissions.

```
Command Prompt                                    _ □ ×
C:\MyPrograms>c++ append.cpp -o append.exe
C:\MyPrograms>append
```

```
poem.txt - Notepad
File  Edit  Format  View  Help
        I never saw a man who looked
        with such a wistful eye
        Upon that little tent of blue
        which prisoners call the sky

        The Ballad of Reading Gaol
                        Oscar Wilde 1898
```

# Reading characters & lines

The **ifstream** filestream object has a **get()** function that can be used in a loop to read a file and assign each character in turn to the **char** variable specified as its argument:

read.cpp

**1** Start a new program by specifying the C++ library classes to include and a namespace prefix to use
```
#include <fstream>      // Include filestream support.
#include <iostream>
using namespace std ;
```

**2** Add a main function containing a final return statement and two variable declarations – one variable to store a character and another to count loop iterations
```
int main()
{
  char letter ;
  int i ;
  // Add more statements here.
  return 0 ;
}
```

**3** In the main function, create an input filestream object to read the text file from the previous example
```
ifstream reader( "poem.txt" ) ;
```

**4** Insert statements to exit unless the filestream object exists
```
if( ! reader )
{
  cout << "Error opening input file" << endl ;
  return -1 ;      // Signal an error then exit the program.
}
```

**5** Next insert a loop to read the text file, assigning each character in turn to the variable and outputting its value
```
for( i = 0 ; ! reader.eof() ; i++ )
{
  reader.get( letter ) ;
  cout << letter ;
}
```

**6** Finally, insert statements to close the filestream, output the total number of loop iterations
```
reader.close() ;
cout << "Iterations: " << i << endl ;
```

7. Save, compile, and run the program to see the text file contents and loop count get displayed on standard output

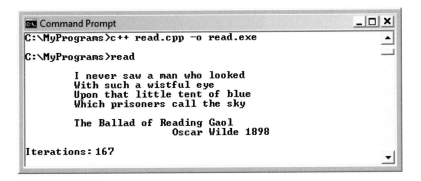

This program works well enough but the loop must make many iterations to output the text file contents. Efficiency could be improved by reading a line on each iteration of the loop:

8. Insert a preprocessor directive to make the C++ string library available to the program
**#include <string>**

9. Replace the character variable declaration with a string variable declaration
**string line ;**

10. Replace both statements in the while loop to read lines, then save, compile, and run the program once more
**getline( reader , line ) ;**
**cout << line << endl ;**

**Don't forget**

Output an **endl** after each line output – because **getline()** stops reading when it meets a \n newline character.

# Formatting with getline

The **getline()** function can optionally have a third argument to specify a delimiter at which to stop reading a line. This can be used to separate text read from a tabulated list in a data file:

format.cpp

1  In a plain text editor, create a text file containing 12 items of data of four items per line, each separated by a tab

2  Start a new program by specifying the C++ library classes to include and a namespace prefix to use
```
#include <fstream>      // Include filestream support.
#include <string>
#include <iostream>
using namespace std ;
```

3  Add a main function containing a final return statement and four variable declarations – a fixed number, a string array to store data, and two counter variables set to zero
```
int main()
{
  const int RANGE = 12 ;
  string tab[ RANGE ] ;
  int i = 0 , j = 0 ;
  // Add more statements here.
  return 0 ;
}
```

## Don't forget

The **string** array must have a sufficient number of elements to store each item of data – it would need to be enlarged to handle more records.

4  Insert a statement to create an input filestream object
```
ifstream reader( "records.txt" ) ;
```

5  Insert statements to exit unless the filestream object exists
```
if( ! reader )
{
  cout << "Error opening input file" << endl ;
  return -1 ;
}
```

**6** Next insert a loop that will read each line into the string array – reading up to a \t tab for the first three items and up to a \n newline for the fourth item on each line

```
while( ! reader.eof() )
{
  if ( ( i + 1 ) % 4 == 0 )
        getline( reader, tab[ i++ ], '\n' ) ;
  else
        getline( reader, tab[ i++ ], '\t' ) ;
}
```

**Hot tip**

The **if** statement tests if the item number (element number plus 1) is exactly divisible by four to determine whether to read up to a newline or tab character.

**7** Now close the filestream and reset the counter

```
reader.close() ;
i = 0 ;
```

**8** Insert a second loop to output the data stored in each array element, formatted with descriptions and newlines

```
while( i < RANGE )
{
  cout << endl << "Record Number: " << ++j << endl ;
  cout << "Forename: " << tab[ i++ ] << endl ;
  cout << "Surname: "  << tab[ i++ ] << endl ;
  cout << "Department: " << tab[ i++ ] << endl ;
  cout << "Telephone: " << tab[ i++ ] << endl ;
}
```

**9** Save, compile, and run the program to see the formatted output from the text file

**Beware**

The record counter must use a prefix incrementer to increase the variable value before it is output.

```
Command Prompt                                    _ □ ×
C:\MyPrograms>c++ format.cpp -o format.exe

C:\MyPrograms>format

Record Number: 1
Forename: John
Surname: Smith
Department: Sales
Telephone: 555-1234

Record Number: 2
Forename: Mary
Surname: Jones
Department: Wages
Telephone: 555-9876

Record Number: 3
Forename: Paul
Surname: Harris
Department: Accts
Telephone: 555-4321

C:\MyPrograms>_
```

# Manipulating input & output

The behavior of input and output streams can be modified using "insertion operators" with the **cout** and **cin** functions. Specifying an integer argument to their **width()** function sets the stream character width. Where the content does not fill the entire stream width a fill character may be specified as the argument to their **fill()** function to indicate the empty portion. Similarly, the default precision of six decimal places for floating point numbers can be changed by specifying an integer to their **precision()** function. Statements using insertion operators to modify a stream should be made before those using the **<<** or **>>** operators.

The **<iostream>** library provides the "manipulators" listed in the table below, which modify a stream using the **<<** or **>>** operators.

88

| Manipulator | Display |
| --- | --- |
| **noboolalpha*** | Boolean values as 1 or 0 |
| **boolalpha** | Boolean values as "true" or "false" |
| **dec*** | Integers as base 10 (decimal) |
| **hex** | Integers as base 16 (hexadecimal) |
| **oct** | Integers as base 8 (octal) |
| **right*** | Text right-justified in the output width |
| **left** | Text left-justified in the output width |
| **internal** | Sign left-justified, number right-justified |
| **noshowbase*** | No prefix indicating numeric base |
| **showbase** | Prefix indicating numeric base |
| **noshowpoint*** | Whole number only when a fraction is zero |
| **showpoint** | Decimal point for all floating point numbers |
| **noshowpos*** | No + prefix before positive numbers |
| **showpos** | Prefix positive numbers with a + sign |
| **noskipws*** | Do not skip whitespace for >> input |
| **skipws** | Skip whitespace for >> input |
| **fixed*** | Floating point numbers to six decimal places |
| **scientific** | Floating point numbers in scientific notation |
| **nouppercase*** | Scientific as e and hexadecimal number as ff |
| **uppercase** | Scientific as E and hexadecimal number as FF |

**1** Start a new program by specifying the C++ library classes to include and a namespace prefix to use
```cpp
#include <iostream>
using namespace std ;
```

manipulate.cpp

**2** Add a main function containing a final return statement and declaring two initialized variables
```cpp
int main()
{
  bool isTrue = 1 ;
  int num = 255 ;
  // Add more statements here.
  return 0 ;
}
```

**3** In the main function, insert statements to set the width and fill of an output stream then output a text string on it
```cpp
cout.width( 40 ) ;
cout.fill( '.' ) ;
cout << "Output" << endl ;
```

**4** Next insert statements to set the precision of an output stream to stop truncation of decimal places – then output a floating point number showing all its decimal places
```cpp
cout.precision(11) ;
cout << "Pi: " << 3.1415926536 << endl ;
```

**5** Now insert statements that use manipulators to output the variable values in modified formats
```cpp
cout << isTrue << ": " << boolalpha << isTrue << endl ;
cout << num << ": " << hex << showbase
                        << uppercase << num << endl ;
```

**Beware**

Manipulators affect all input or output on that stream. For example, the **boolalpha** manipulator will display all boolean values on that stream in written form.

**6** Save, compile, and run the program to see the output

```
Command Prompt                                    _ □ ×

C:\MyPrograms>c++ manipulate.cpp -o manipulate.exe

C:\MyPrograms>manipulate
........................................Output
Pi: 3.1415926536
1: true
255: 0XFF

C:\MyPrograms>_
```

# Predicting problems

Despite the best efforts of the programmer C++ programs may unfortunately contain one, or more, of these three types of bugs:

- **Syntax errors** – the code contains incorrect use of the C++ language. For example, an opening brace does not have a matching closing brace.

- **Logic errors** – the code is syntactically correct but attempts to perform an operation that is illegal. For example, the program may attempt to divide a number by zero, causing an error.

- **Exception errors** – the program runs as expected until an exceptional condition is encountered that crashes the program. For example, the program may request a number, which the user enters in word form rather than in numeric form.

The C++ standards allow the compiler to spot "compile-time" errors involving syntax and logic but the possibility of exceptional errors is more difficult to locate as they only occur at "run-time". This means that the programmer must try to predict problems that may arise and prepare to handle those exceptional errors.

The first step is to identify which part of the program code that may, under certain conditions, cause an exception error. This can then be surrounded by a "try" block, which uses the **try** keyword and encloses the suspect code within a pair of braces.

When an exception error occurs the **try** block then "throws" the exception out to a "catch" block, which immediately follows the **try** block. This uses the **catch** keyword and encloses statements to handle the exception error within a pair of braces.

The program described on the opposite page has a **try** block containing a loop that increments an integer. When the integer reaches five a **throw()** function manually throws an exception to the **catch** block exception handler, passing the integer argument.

## Hot tip

Always consider that the user will perform the unexpected – then ensure your programs can handle those actions.

**1** Start a new program by specifying the C++ library classes to include and a namespace prefix to use

```
#include <iostream>
using namespace std ;
```

try.cpp

**2** Add a main function containing a final return statement and declaring an integer variable for increment by a loop

```
int main()
{
  int number ;
  // Add more statements here.
  return 0 ;
}
```

**3** In the main function, insert try and catch blocks to handle a "bad number" exception

```
try
{       }
catch( int num )
{       }
```

**4** In the try block, insert a loop to increment the variable

```
for( number = 1 ; number < 21 ; number++ )
{
  if (number > 4 ) throw( number ) ;
  else
  cout << "Number: " << number << endl ;
}
```

**5** In the catch block, insert an exception handler statement

```
cout << "Exception at: " << num << endl ;
```

**6** Save, compile, and run the program to see the thrown exception get caught by the catch block

**Don't forget**

When an exception occurs control passes to the **catch** block – in this example the loop does not complete.

```
Command Prompt                                    _ □ ×

C:\MyPrograms>c++ try.cpp -o try.exe

C:\MyPrograms>try
Number: 1
Number: 2
Number: 3
Number: 4
Exception at: 5

C:\MyPrograms>_
```

# Recognizing exceptions

When a program exception occurs within a **try** block an "exception" object is automatically thrown. A reference to the exception can be passed to the associated **catch** block in the parentheses after the **catch** keyword. This specifies the argument to be an **exception** type, and a chosen exception name prefixed by the **&** reference operator. For example, **exception &error** .

Once an exception reference is passed to a **catch** block an error description can be retrieved by the exception's **what()** function:

what.cpp

**1** Start a new program by specifying the C++ library classes to include and a namespace prefix to use
```
#include <string>                    // Include string support.
#include <iostream>
using namespace std ;
```

**2** Add a main function containing a final return statement and declaring an initialized string variable
```
int main()
{
  string lang = "C++" ;
  // Add more statements here.
  return 0 ;
}
```

**3** In the main function, insert a try block containing a statement attempting to erase part of the string variable
```
try{      lang.erase( 4, 6 ) ;          }
```

**Don't forget**

The error description will vary for different compilers – the Visual C++ compiler describes the exception error in this example as an "invalid string position".

**4** Next insert a catch block containing a statement to send a description to standard error output by the cerr function
```
catch( exception &error )
{ cerr << "Exception: " << error.what() << endl ;         }
```

**5** Save, compile, and run the program to see the error description of the caught exception

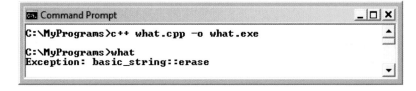

```
C:\MyPrograms>c++ what.cpp -o what.exe

C:\MyPrograms>what
Exception: basic_string::erase
```

92

The C++ **<stdexcept>** library defines a number of exception classes. Its base class is named "exception" from which other classes are derived, categorizing common exceptions.

Each of the exception classes are listed in the table below, illustrating their relationship and describing their exception type:

| Exception class | Description |
|---|---|
| exception | General exception |
| — bad_alloc | failure allocating storage |
| — bad_cast | failure casting data type |
| — bad_typeid | failure referencing typeid |
| — logic_error | Logic exception |
|    domain_error | invalid domain |
|    invalid_argument | invalid argument in call |
|    length_error | invalid length for container |
|    out_of_range | invalid element range |
| — runtime_error | Runtime exception |
|    range_error | invalid range request |
|    overflow_error | invalid arithmetic request |

**Don't forget**

The **cout** function sends data to standard output, whereas the **cerr** function sends error data to standard error output. These are simply two different data streams.

When the **<stdexcept>** library is made available to a program, by adding an **#include <stdexcept>** preprocessor directive, the exception classes can be used to identify the type of exception thrown to a **catch** block.

The specific exception class name can appear, in place of the general **exception** type, within the **catch** block's parentheses.

Multiple **catch** blocks can be used in succession, much like **case** statements in a **switch** block, to handle several types of exception.

Additionally, exceptions can be produced manually by the **throw** keyword. This can be used to create any of the **logic_error** and **runtime_error** exceptions in the table above. Optionally, a custom error message can be specified for manual exceptions, which can be retrieved by its **what()** function.

**Hot tip**

The example described on the next page demonstrates the use of standard exceptions.

# Handling errors

Error handling in C++ is performed using the **try**, **catch**, and **throw** keywords to handle the program exceptions described on the previous page:

except.cpp

**1**   Start a new program by specifying the C++ library classes to include and a namespace prefix to use
```
#include <stdexcept>   // Support standard exceptions.
#include <fstream>
#include <string>
#include <iostream>
using namespace std ;
```

**2**   Add a main function containing a final return statement, two initialized variable declarations, and a statement ouputting a text message
```
int main()
{
  string lang = "C++" ;
  int num = 1000000000 ;         // One billion.
  // Try-catch block goes here.
  cout << "Program continues..." << endl ;
  return 0 ;
}
```

**3**   In the main function, insert a try block containing a statement attempting to replace part of the string value
```
try { lang.replace( 100, 1 , "C" ) ;          }
```

**4**   After the try block, add a catch block to handle a range exception then save, compile, and run the program
```
catch( out_of_range &e )
{
  cerr << "Range Exception: " << e.what() << endl ;
  cerr << "Exception Type: " << typeid( e ).name() ;
  cerr << endl << "Program terminated." << endl ;
  return -1 ;
}
```

## Don't forget

The **out_of_range** error occurs because the **replace()** function is trying to begin erasing at the 100th character, but the **string** variable has only three characters.

```
Command Prompt                                              _ □ ×

C:\MyPrograms>c++ except.cpp -o except.exe

C:\MyPrograms>except
Range Exception: basic_string::replace
Exception Type: St12out_of_range
Program terminated.
```

**5** Replace the statement in the **try** block with one attempting to resize the **string** variable
**lang.resize( 3 * num ) ;**

**6** After the **catch** block, add a second **catch** block to handle general exceptions
```
catch( exception &e )
{
  cerr << "Exception: " << e.what() << endl ;
  cerr << "Exception Type: " << typeid( e ).name()
                                        << endl ;
}
```

**Beware**

The order of **catch** blocks can be important – placing the **exception** error handler before the **out_of_range** error handler would allow an **out_of_range** error to be handled by the (higher level) **exception** handler.

**7** Save, compile, and run the program again to see the exception handled by the second **catch** block

```
Command Prompt                                    _ □ ×

C:\MyPrograms>c++ except.cpp -o except.exe

C:\MyPrograms>except
Exception: basic_string::resize
Exception Type: St12length_error
Program continues...

C:\MyPrograms>_
```

**8** Replace the statement in the **try** block with one attempting to open a non-existent file
**ifstream reader( "nonsuch.txt" ) ;**
**if( ! reader ) throw logic_error("File not found" );**

**Hot tip**

An exception object is typically given the name "e" – as seen here.

**9** Save, compile, and run the program once more to see the exception handled again by the second **catch** block, and the specified custom error message

```
Command Prompt                                    _ □ ×

C:\MyPrograms>c++ except.cpp -o except.exe

C:\MyPrograms>except
Exception: File not found
Exception Type: St11logic_error
Program continues...

C:\MyPrograms>_
```

# Summary

- The C++ **<fstream>** library provides functions for working with files as **ifstream** input or **ofstream** output stream objects

- Upon completion a stream's **close()** function should be called

- File modes can be used to control the behavior of a stream

- An input stream's **get()** function reads one character at a time

- The **getline()** function can be used to read a line at a time from an input stream

- Optionally, the **getline()** function can have a third argument specifying a delimiter character at which to stop reading

- Insertion operators can be used with the **cin** and **cout** functions to modify their behavior

- The **cout.width()** function sets the width of the output stream

- The **cout.fill()** function specifies a character to occupy any empty portion of the output

- The **cout.precision()** function determines how many decimal places to display when the output is a floating point number

- A badly performing program may contain syntax errors, logic errors, or exception errors

- A **try** block can be used to enclose statements that, under certain conditions, may cause an exception error

- A **catch** block can be used to handle exception errors produced in its associated **try** block

- Exception errors that occur in a **try** block are automatically thrown to the associated **catch** block

- Exceptions can be manually thrown to the associated catch block using the **throw()** function

- The C++ **<stdexcept>** library defines a number of exception classes that categorize common exceptions

# 6 Pointing to data

*This chapter demonstrates how to produce efficient C++ programs utilizing pointers and references.*

# Understanding data storage

In order to understand C++ pointers it is helpful to understand how data is stored on your computer. Envision the computer's memory as a very long row of sequentially numbered slots, which can each contain one byte of data. When a variable is declared in a program the machine reserves a number of slots at which to store data assigned to that variable. The number of slots it reserves depends upon the variable's data type. When the program uses the variable name to retrieve stored data it actually addresses the number of the variable's first reserved slot.

Comparison can be drawn to a long row of sequentially numbered houses that can each accommodate a different family. Any family can be explicitly referenced by addressing their house number.

The slot (house) numbers in computer memory are expressed in hexadecimal format and can be revealed by the **&** reference operator.

address.cpp

**1** Start a new program by specifying the C++ library classes to include and a namespace prefix to use
```
#include <string>
#include <iostream>
using namespace std ;
```

**2** Add a main function containing a final return statement and declaring three initialized variables
```
int main()
{
  int num = 100 ;
  double sum = 0.0123456789 ;
  string text = "C++ Fun" ;
  // Add more statements here.
  return 0 ;
}
```

**3** In the main function, insert statements to output the memory address of the first slot of each variable
```
cout << "Integer variable starts at: " << &num << endl ;
cout << "Double variable starts at: " << &sum << endl ;
cout << "String variable starts at: " << &text << endl ;
```

**4** Save, compile, and run the program to see the three memory addresses

```
Command Prompt                                          _ |□| X

C:\MyPrograms>c++ address.cpp -o address.exe

C:\MyPrograms>address
Integer variable starts at: 0x22ff3c
Double variable starts at: 0x22ff30
String variable starts at: 0x22ff20

C:\MyPrograms>_
```

Once memory space has been reserved by a variable declaration, a value of the appropriate data type can be stored there using the = assignment operator. For example, **num = 100** takes the value on its right (**100**) and puts it in the memory referenced by the named variable on its left (**num**).

The operand to the left of the = assignment operator called its "L-value" and the operand to its right is called its "R-value". Consider the "L" in L-value to mean "Location" and consider the "R" in R-value to mean "Read".

One important rule in C++ programming insists that an R-value cannot appear to the left of the = assignment operator – but an L-value may appear on either side. Code that places an R-value to the left of an = assignment operator will not compile:

**5**    Just before the return statement, insert statements placing R-values incorrectly to the left of assignment operators
**200 = num ;**
**5.5 = sum ;**
**"Bad assignments" = text ;**

**6**    Save, and attempt to recompile the program to see the errors caused by incorrectly placed R-values

```
Command Prompt                                          _ |□| X

C:\MyPrograms>c++ address.cpp -o address.exe
address.cpp: In function 'int main()':
address.cpp:21: error: non-lvalue in assignment
address.cpp:22: error: non-lvalue in assignment
address.cpp:23: error: assignment of read-only location
address.cpp:23: error: incompatible types in assignment of
 'std::string' to 'const char[16]'

C:\MyPrograms>_
```

Don't forget

The location addresses are dynamically allocated – so will vary from those in this screenshot.

66

Hot tip

L-values are containers but R-values are data.

# Getting values with pointers

Pointers are a useful part of efficient C++ programming – they are simply variables that store the memory address of other variables.

Pointer variables are declared in the same way that other variables are declared, but the data type is suffixed by a "*" character. This denotes, in a declaration, that the variable will be a pointer. Always remember that the pointer's data type must match that of the variable to which it points.

A pointer variable is initialized by assigning it the memory address of another variable using the **&** reference operator. The assignment can be made either in the declaration statement, or in a separate statement after the declaration. Referencing a pointer variable by its name alone will simply reveal the memory address that it contains.

After a pointer variable has been initialized, either in the declaration or by a subsequent assignment, it "points" to the variable at the address which it contains. Usefully, this means that the value of the variable to which it points can be referenced by prefixing the pointer name with the * dereference operator:

deref.cpp

1. Start a new program by specifying the C++ library classes to include and a namespace prefix to use
```
#include <iostream>
using namespace std ;
```

2. Add a main function containing a final return statement and declaring two regular initialized integer variables
```
int main()
{
  int a = 8 , b = 16 ;
  // Add more statements here.
  return 0 ;
}
```

3. In the main function, insert a statement to declare and initialize a pointer with the memory address of the first integer variable
```
int* aPtr = &a ;          // aPtr assigned address of a.
```

**4** Insert a statement to declare a second pointer, then initialize it with the address of the second integer variable

```
int* bPtr ;          // bPtr declared.
bPtr = &b ;          // bPtr assigned address of b.
```

**5** Next insert statements to output the actual memory address of each pointer

```
cout << "Addresses of pointers..." << endl ;
cout << "aPtr: " << &aPtr << endl ;
cout << "bPtr: " << &bPtr << endl << endl ;
```

## Hot tip

The * dereference operator is alternatively known as the "indirection" operator.

**6** Now insert statements to output the memory address stored inside each pointer

```
cout << "Values in pointers..." << endl ;
cout << "aPtr: " << aPtr << endl ;
cout << "bPtr: " << bPtr << endl << endl ;
```

**7** Finally insert statements to output the values stored at the memory address stored in each pointer – the value of the variables to which the pointers point

```
cout << "Values in addresses pointed to..." << endl ;
cout << "a: " << *aPtr << endl ;
cout << "b: " << *bPtr << endl ;
```

**8** Save, compile, and run the program to see the pointer addresses and the stored values

```
Command Prompt                                    _ □ X

C:\MyPrograms>c++ deref.cpp -o deref.exe

C:\MyPrograms>deref
Addresses of pointers...
aPtr: 0x22ff4c
bPtr: 0x22ff48

Values in pointers...
aPtr: 0x22ff54
bPtr: 0x22ff50

Values in addresses pointed to...
a: 8
b: 16


C:\MyPrograms>_
```

## Don't forget

The memory addresses are dynamically allocated – so will vary from those in this screenshot.

# Doing pointer arithmetic

Once a pointer variable has been initialized with a memory address it can be assigned another address, or changed using pointer arithmetic.

The **++** increment operator or the **--** decrement operator will move the pointer along to the next or previous address for that data type – the larger the data type, the bigger the jump.

Even larger jumps can be achieved using the **+=** and **-=** operators.

Pointer arithmetic is especially useful with arrays because the elements in an array occupy consecutive memory addresses. Assigning just the name of an array to a pointer automatically assigns it the address of the first element. Incrementing the pointer by one moves the pointer along to the next element.

point.cpp

1  Start a new program by specifying the C++ library classes to include and a namespace prefix to use
```
#include <iostream>
using namespace std ;
```

2  Add a main function containing a final return statement and declaring an initialized integer array of ten elements
```
int main()
{
  int nums[] = { 1, 2, 3, 4, 5, 6, 7, 8, 9, 10 } ;
  // Add more statements here.
  return 0 ;
}
```

3  In the main function, insert a statement to declare a pointer, initialized with the memory address of the first element in the integer array
```
int* ptr = nums ;
```

4  Next insert a statement to output the memory address of the first element of the integer array, and its value
```
cout << endl << "ptr at: " << ptr << " gets: "<< *ptr ;
```

5  Now increment the pointer and output its new memory address – that of the second element in the integer array
```
ptr++ ;
cout << endl << "ptr at: " << ptr << " gets: "<< *ptr ;
```

**6** Increment the pointer again and output its new memory address – that of the third element in the integer array
```
ptr++ ;
cout << endl << "ptr at: " << ptr << " gets: " << *ptr ;
```

**7** Decrement the pointer by two places and output its memory address – that of the first element in the array
```
ptr -= 2 ;
cout << endl << "ptr at: " << ptr << " gets: " << *ptr ;
cout << endl ;
```

### Beware

The *=, /=, and %= operators cannot be used to move a pointer.

**8** Now insert a loop to output the value stored in each element of the integer array
```
for( int i = 0 ; i < 10 ; i++ )
{
        cout << endl << "Element: " << i ;
        cout << "    Value: " << *ptr ;
        ptr++ ;
}
cout << endl ;
```

**9** Save, compile, and run the program to see the pointer addresses and the stored values

```
 Command Prompt                                    _ □ X

C:\MyPrograms>c++ point.cpp -o point.exe

C:\MyPrograms>point

ptr at: 0x22ff20 gets: 1
ptr at: 0x22ff24 gets: 2
ptr at: 0x22ff28 gets: 3
ptr at: 0x22ff20 gets: 1

Element: 0    Value: 1
Element: 1    Value: 2
Element: 2    Value: 3
Element: 3    Value: 4
Element: 4    Value: 5
Element: 5    Value: 6
Element: 6    Value: 7
Element: 7    Value: 8
Element: 8    Value: 9
Element: 9    Value: 10

C:\MyPrograms>_
```

### Hot tip

The name of an array acts like a pointer to its first element.

# Passing pointers to functions

Pointers can access the data stored in the variable to which they point using the * dereference operator. This can also be used to change the stored data by assigning a new value of the appropriate data type.

Additionally, pointers can be passed to functions as arguments – with a subtly different effect to passing variables as arguments:

● When variables are passed to functions their data is passed "by value" to a local variable inside the function – so that the function operates on a <u>copy</u> of the original value.

● When pointers are passed to functions their data is passed "by reference" – so that the function operates on the <u>original</u> value.

The benefit of passing by reference allows functions to directly manipulate variable values declared within the calling function.

fnptr.cpp

1 Start a new program by specifying the C++ library classes to include and a namespace prefix to use
```
#include <iostream>
using namespace std ;
```

2 After the preprocessor instructions, declare two function prototypes to each accept a single pointer argument
```
void writeOutput( int* ) ;
void computeTriple( int* ) ;
```

3 Add a main function containing a final return statement and declaring an initialized regular integer variable
```
int main()
{
  int num = 5 ;
  // Add more statements here.
  return 0 ;
}
```

4 In the main function, insert a second variable declaration that initializes a pointer with the address of the regular integer variable
```
int* ptr = &num ;
```

**5** After the main function block, define a function to output the current value of a variable to which a pointer points
```
void writeOutput( int* value )
{
  cout << "Current value: " << *value << endl ;
}
```

**Don't forget**

The function prototype and definition must both contain a pointer argument.

**6** Define another function to multiply the current value of a variable to which a pointer points
```
void computeTriple( int* value )
{
  *value *= 3 ;  // Multiply and assign dereferenced value.
}
```

**7** In the main function, pass a pointer argument to a function to output the variable value to which it points
```
writeOutput( ptr ) ;
```

**8** Next use the pointer to increase the variable value, then display its new value
```
*ptr += 15 ;    // Add and assign a dereferenced value.
writeOutput( ptr ) ;
```

**9** Now pass a pointer argument to a function to multiply the variable to which it points, then display its new value
```
computeTriple( ptr ) ;
writeOutput( ptr ) ;
```

**10** Save, compile, and run the program to see the computed values output

**Hot tip**

Functions that operate directly on variables within the calling function need no return statement.

# Making arrays of pointers

A variable of the regular **char** data type can be assigned a single character value but a pointer to a **char** array can usefully be assigned a string of characters. The string is actually stored as an array of characters, with one character per element, but referencing the **char** pointer will automatically retrieve the entire string.

This ability to retrieve a string value from a **char** pointer using just its variable name resembles the way that a string can be retrieved from a regular **char** array using its variable name.

Multiple strings can be stored in a **char** pointer array, with one string per element. You can even store multiple **char** pointer arrays in a "master" **char** pointer array, with one array per element.

arrptr.cpp

1. Start a new program by specifying the C++ library classes to include and a namespace prefix to use
   ```
   #include <iostream>
   using namespace std ;
   ```

2. Add a main function containing a final return statement and declaring two initialized variables – a regular character array, and a character pointer with identical string values
   ```
   int main()
   {
     char letters[ 8 ] = { 'C', '+' , '+' , ' ' , 'F', 'u', 'n', '\0' } ;
     char* text = "C++ Fun" ;
     // Add more statements here.
     return 0 ;
   }
   ```

### Don't forget

Character values must be enclosed in single quotes, but string values must be enclosed in double quotes – even when it is being assigned to a **char** pointer.

3. In the main function, insert statements to declare and initialize two further character pointer variables, with unique string values
   ```
   char* term = "Element" ;
   char* lang = "C++" ;
   ```

4. Next insert a statement to declare a character pointer array initialized with three string values
   ```
   char* ap1[ 3 ] = { "Great " , "Program" , "Code   " } ;
   ```

**5** Now insert a statement to declare a second character pointer array initialized with three string values – making one of the pointer variables its first element value
**char\* ap2[ 3 ] = { lang , "is " , "Fun" } ;**

**6** Declare two "master" character pointer arrays, each initialized with three elements of the **char** pointer arrays
**char\* ap3[ 3 ] = { ap2[ 0 ] , ap2[ 1 ] , ap1[ 0 ] } ;**
**char\* ap4[ 3 ] = { ap1[ 2 ] , ap2[ 1 ] , ap2[ 2 ] } ;**

**7** After the declarations, insert statements to output the identical string values of the first two variables
**cout << letters << endl ;**
**cout << text << endl ;**

**8** Next insert a loop containing a statement to output the value within a character pointer and the iteration number
**for( int i = 0 ; i < 3 ; i++ )**
**{**
**  cout << term << i << "   ";**
**}**

**9** Within the loop block, insert statements to output each element value of the four character pointer arrays
**cout << ap1[ i ] << "   " ;**
**cout << ap2[ i ] << "   " ;**
**cout << ap3[ i ] << "   " ;**
**cout << ap4[ i ] << endl ;**

**10** Save, compile, and run the program to see the character string output

### Don't forget

To include a space in a **char** array the assignment must have a space between the quotes as ' ' – two single quotes together ( '' ) is regarded as an empty element and causes a compiler error.

### Beware

Remember that the final element of a **char** array must contain the special \0 character to designate that array as a string.

```
Command Prompt                                    _ □ ✕

C:\MyPrograms>c++ arrptr.cpp -o arrptr.exe

C:\MyPrograms>arrptr
C++ Fun
C++ Fun
Element:0        Great   C++     C++     Code
Element:1        Program is      is      is
Element:2        Code    Fun     Great   Fun

C:\MyPrograms>_
```

# Referencing data

A C++ "reference" is an alias for a variable or an object in a program. A reference <u>must</u> be initialized within its declaration, by assigning it the name of the variable or object to which it refers. From then on the reference acts as an alternative name for the item to which it refers – anything that happens to the reference is really implemented on the variable or object to which it refers.

A reference declaration first states its data type, matching that of the item to which it will refer, suffixed by an **&** character denoting that variable will be a reference, and a chosen name. Finally the declaration uses the = operator to associate a variable or object.

Traditionally, a reference is named with the name of the associated variable or object but with an uppercase first letter and the whole name prefixed by an "r". For example, a declaration to create a reference to an integer variable named "num" looks like this:

**int& rNum = num ;**

Note that the purpose of the **&** reference operator is context-sensitive so that it declares a reference when used as an L-value, on the left side of the = operator, otherwise it returns a memory address when used as an R-value.

A reference is such a true alias to its associated item that querying its memory address returns the address of its associated item – there is no way to discover the address of the reference itself.

## Beware

Once a reference has been created it will always refer to the item to which it was initialized – a different item cannot be assigned to that reference.

ref.cpp

1  Start a new program by specifying the C++ library classes
   to include and a namespace prefix to use
   **#include <iostream>**
   **using namespace std ;**

2  Add a main function containing a final return statement
   and declaring two variables – a regular integer variable
   and a reference to that variable
   **int main()**
   **{**
     **int num ;**
     **int& rNum = num ;**
     // Add more statements here.
     **return 0 ;**
   **}**

...cont'd

3    In the main function, insert a statement assigning an initial value to the integer variable via its reference

**rNum = 400 ;**

4    Next insert statements to output the stored value, both directly and via its reference

**cout << "Value direct: " << num << endl ;**

**cout << "Value via reference: " << rNum << endl ;**

5    Now insert statements to output the memory address, both directly and via its reference

**cout << "Address direct: " << &num << endl ;**

**cout << "Address via reference: " << &rNum << endl ;**

6    Insert a statement to manipulate the value stored in the variable via its reference

**rNum *= 2 ;**

7    Once more output the stored value, both directly and via its reference

**cout << "Value direct: " << num << endl ;**

**cout << "Value via reference: " << rNum << endl ;**

8    Save, compile, and run the program to see the values and memory address

**Beware**

The compiler decides how to use the **&** reference operator according to its context.

```
C:\MyPrograms>c++ ref.cpp -o ref.exe

C:\MyPrograms>ref
Value direct: 400
Value via reference: 400
Address direct: 0x22ff54
Address via reference: 0x22ff54
Value direct: 800
Value via reference: 800

C:\MyPrograms>_
```

**Don't forget**

A reference is always an alias for the item associated in its declaration statement.

# Passing references to functions

References provide access to the data stored in the variable to which they refer, just like the variable itself, and can be used to change the stored data by assigning a new value of the appropriate data type.

Additionally, references can, like pointers, be passed to functions as arguments:

● When variables are passed to functions their data is passed "by value" to a local variable inside the function – so that the function operates on a <u>copy</u> of the original value.

● When references are passed to functions their data is passed "by reference" – so the function operates on the <u>original</u> value.

The benefit of passing by reference allows functions to directly manipulate variable values declared within the calling function.

fnref.cpp

### Hot tip

This example may seem familiar as it recreates the example on page 104 – but replaces pointers with references.

**1** Start a new program by specifying the C++ library classes to include and a namespace prefix to use
```
#include <iostream>
using namespace std ;
```

**2** After the preprocessor instructions, declare two function prototypes to each accept a single reference argument
```
void writeOutput( int& ) ;
void computeTriple( int& ) ;
```

**3** Add a main function containing a final return statement and declaring an initialized regular integer variable
```
int main()
{
  int num = 5 ;
  // Add more statements here.
  return 0 ;
}
```

**4** In the main function, insert a second variable declaration, initializing a reference as an alias of the integer variable
```
int& ref = num ;
```

**5** After the main function block, define a function to output the current value of a variable to which a reference refers

```
void writeOutput( int& value )
{
  cout << "Current value: " << value << endl ;
}
```

**6** Define another function to multiply the current value of a variable to which a reference refers

```
void computeTriple( int& value )
{
  value *= 3 ;   // Multiply and assign a referenced value.
}
```

**7** In the main function, pass a reference argument to a function to output the variable value to which it refers

```
writeOutput( ref ) ;
```

**8** Next use the reference to increase the variable value, then display its new value

```
ref += 15 ;   // Add and assign a referenced value.
writeOutput( ref ) ;
```

**9** Now pass a reference argument to a function to multiply the variable to which it refers, then display its new value

```
computeTriple( ref ) ;
writeOutput( ref ) ;
```

**10** Save, compile, and run the program to see the computed values output

# Comparing pointers & references

Pointers and references can both be used to refer to variable values and to pass them to functions by reference rather than by value. Technically, passing by reference is more efficient than passing by value so the use of pointers and references is to be encouraged.

The decision whether to use a pointer or a reference is determined by the program requirements. C++ programmers generally prefer to use references wherever possible as they are easier to use and easier to understand than pointers. References must, however, obey certain rules which can make the use of pointers necessary:

| Rule | References | Pointers |
|---|---|---|
| Can be declared without initialization | No | Yes |
| Can be reassigned | No | Yes |
| Can contain a 0 (null) value | No | Yes |
| Easiest to use | Yes | No |

As a general rule the choice between using a reference or a pointer can be determined by following these guidelines:

● If you don't want to initialize in the declaration use a pointer

OR

● If you want to be able to reassign another variable use a pointer

OTHERWISE

● Always use a reference

Pointers are more flexible than references, however, and can even point to functions. In this case the pointer declaration must precisely match the return data type and arguments to those of the function to which it points. Additionally the pointer name must be enclosed within parentheses in the declaration to avoid compiler errors. The function pointer can then be assigned a function by name so that function can be called via the pointer.

### Don't forget

A reference must be initialized in the declaration to refer to a variable or object – then always refers to that item.

① Start a new program by specifying the C++ library classes to include and a namespace prefix to use

```cpp
#include <iostream>
using namespace std ;
```

pref.cpp

② After the preprocessor instructions, define an inline function to output the total of two passed arguments

```cpp
void add( int& a, int* b )
{ cout << "Total: " << ( a + *b ) << endl ; } ;
```

③ Add a main function containing a final return statement and declarations creating two regular integer variables, one reference, and two pointers

```cpp
int main()
{
  int num = 100 , sum = 500 ;
  int& rNum = num ;
  int* ptr = &num ;
  void (* fn) ( int& a, int* b ) = add ;
  // Add more statements here.
  return 0 ;
}
```

④ In the main function, insert statements to output the first integer variable values via the reference and pointer

```cpp
cout << "Reference: " << rNum << endl ;
cout << "Pointer: " << *ptr << endl ;
```

⑤ Now assign the second integer variable to the pointer and output its value via the pointer, then call the function pointer to output the sum of the variable values

```cpp
ptr = &sum ;
cout << "Pointer now: " << *ptr <, endl ;
add( rNum , ptr ) ;
```

⑥ Save, compile, and run the program to see the output

```
Command Prompt                               _ □ ×
C:\MyPrograms>c++ pref.cpp -o pref.exe
C:\MyPrograms>pref
Reference: 100
Pointer: 100
Pointer now: 500
Total: 600
```

113

### Hot tip

C programmers tend to put the & and * characters before the variable names but in C++ it is usual to put them after the data type – as the feature is a property of the data type, not the name.

# Summary

- Data is stored in computer memory within sequentially numbered addresses

- Operands to the left of an = operator are L-values, and those to its right are R-values

- An R-value may only appear to the right of an = operator

- A pointer is a variable that stores the memory address of another variable – that to which it points

- The * character appears as an L-value in a pointer declaration indicating that the statement will create a pointer variable

- Once declared, the * dereference operator can be used to reference the value within a variable to which a pointer points

- Pointer arithmetic can be used to iterate through the values stored in array elements

- A variable is passed to a function by value, whereas pointers and references are passed by reference

- Passing by reference allows the receiving function to directly manipulate variables declared within the calling function

- A string value can be assigned to a pointer of the **char** data type, and the whole string retrieved using the pointer name

- Each element in a pointer array can store data or a pointer

- A reference is not a variable, but merely an alias for a variable

- The **&** character appears as an L-value in a reference declaration indicating that the statement will create an alias

- The **&** reference operator can be used to reference the memory address stored within a pointer

- References are easier to use than pointers but, unlike pointers, a reference must always be initialized in its declaration and can never be assigned a different variable

# 7

# Creating classes and objects

*This chapter introduces the topics of encapsulation and inheritance – the first two principles of Object Oriented Programming.*

# Encapsulating data

A class is a data structure that can contain both variables and functions in a single entity. These are collectively known as its "members", and the functions are known as its "methods".

Access to class members from outside the class is controlled by "access specifiers" in the class declaration. Typically these will deny access to the variable members but allow access to methods that can store and retrieve data from those variable members. This technique of "data hiding" ensures that stored data is safely encapsulated within the class variable members and is the first principle of Object Oriented Programming (OOP).

A class declaration begins with the **class** keyword, followed by a space, then a programmer-specified name – adhering to the usual C++ naming conventions but beginning in uppercase. Next come the access specifiers and class members, contained within a pair of braces. Every class declaration must end with a semicolon after the closing brace – so the class declaration syntax looks like this:

```
class ClassName
{
  access specifier :
    member1 ;
    member2 ;
  access specifier :
    member3 ;
    member4 ;
} ;
```

### Don't forget

Derived classes, which use the **protected** access specifier, are introduced later in this chapter.

An access specifier may be any one of the keywords **public, private,** or **protected** to specify access rights for its listed members:

● Public members are accessible from any place where the class is visible

● Private members are accessible only to other members of the same class

● Protected members are accessible only to other members of the same class and to members of classes derived from that class

By default, all class members have private access – so any members that appear in the class declaration without an access specifier will have private access.

Any real-world object can be defined by its attributes and by its actions. For example, a dog has attributes such as age, weight, and color and actions it can perform such as bark. The class mechanism in C++ provides a way to create a virtual dog object within a program, where the variable members of a class can represent its attributes and the methods represent its actions:

```
class Dog
{
  private: // The default access level.
    int age, weight ;
    string color ;
  public :
    void bark() ;
    // ... Plus methods to store/retrieve data.
} ;
```

**Don't forget**

While a program class cannot perfectly emulate a real-word object the aim is to encapsulate all relevant attributes and actions.

It is important to recognize that a class declaration only defines a data structure – in order to create an object you must declare an "instance" of that data structure. This is achieved in just the same way that instances are declared of regular C++ data types:

```
int num ;        // Creates an instance named "num".
                 // of the regular C++ int data type.

Dog fido ;       // Creates an instance named "fido".
                 // of the programmer-defined Dog data structure.
```

Alternatively, an instance object can be created by specifying its name between the class declaration's closing brace and its final semicolon. Multiple instances can be created this way by specifying a comma-separated list of object names. For example, the class declaration listed below creates four instance objects of the Dog class named "fido", "pooch", "rex", and "sammy".

**Hot tip**

It is conventional to begin class names with an uppercase character and object names with lowercase.

```
class Dog
{
    int age, weight ;
    string color ;
  public:
    void bark() ;
    // ... Plus methods to store/retrieve data.
} fido, pooch, rex, sammy ;
```

The principle of encapsulation in C++ programming describes the grouping together of data and functionality in class members – age, weight, color attributes and bark action in the Dog class.

117

# Creating an object

In order to assign and retrieve data from private members of a class, special public accessor methods must be added to the class. These are "setter" methods, to assign data, and "getter" methods, to retrieve data. Accessor methods are often named as the variable they address, with the first letter made uppercase, and prefixed by "set" or "get" respectively. For example, accessor methods to address an **age** variable may be named **setAge()** and **getAge()**.

object.cpp

**Don't forget**

Members declared before an access specifier are private by default, and remember to add a final semicolon after each class declaration.

**Hot tip**

In the class declaration, notice that all methods are declared public and all variables are declared private. This notion of "public interface, private data" is a key concept when creating classes.

1. Start a new program by specifying the C++ library classes to include and a namespace prefix to use
```
#include <string>
#include <iostream>
using namespace std ;
```

2. Declare a class named "Dog"
```
class Dog
{

} ;
```

3. Between the braces of the Dog class declaration, declare three private variable members
```
int age, weight ;
string color ;
```

4. After the private variables, add a public access specifier
```
public:
```

5. Begin the public members list by adding a method to output a string when called
```
void bark() { cout << "WOOF!" << endl ; }
```

6. Add public setter methods – to assign individual values to each of the private variables
```
void setAge( int yrs )    { age = yrs ;    }
void setWeight( int lbs ) { weight = lbs ; }
void setColor( string clr ) { color = clr ;  }
```

7. Add public methods – to retrieve individual values from each of the private variables
```
int getAge()    { return age ;    }
int getWeight() { return weight ; }
string getColor() { return color ; }
```

**8** After the Dog class declaration, declare a main method containing a final return statement

```
int main()
{
  // Program code goes here.
  return 0 ;
}
```

**9** Between the braces of the main method, declare an instance of the Dog class named "fido"

```
Dog fido ;
```

**10** Add statements calling each setter method to assign data

```
fido.setAge( 3 ) ;
fido.setWeight( 15 ) ;
fido.setColor( "brown" ) ;
```

**11** Add statements calling each getter method to retrieve the assigned values

```
cout << "Fido is a " << fido.getColor() <<
                             " dog" << endl ;
cout << "Fido is " << fido.getAge() <<
                        " years old" << endl ;
cout << "Fido weighs " << fido.getWeight() <<
                            " pounds" << endl ;
```

**12** Now add a call to the regular output method

```
fido.bark() ;
```

**13** Save, compile, and run the program to see the output

```
C:\MyPrograms>c++ object.cpp -o object.exe

C:\MyPrograms>object
Fido is a brown dog
Fido is 3 years old
Fido weighs 15 pounds
WOOF!

C:\MyPrograms>_
```

Fido

**Hot tip**

This program will get modified over the next few pages as new features are incorporated.

# Creating multiple objects

A program can easily create multiple objects simply by declaring multiple instances of a class, and each object can have unique attributes by assigning individual values with its setter methods.

It is often convenient to combine the setter methods into a single method that accepts arguments for each private variable. This means that all values can be assigned with a single statement in the program, but the method will contain multiple statements.

The class declaration in the previous example contains short methods of just one line, which are created "inline" – entirely within the class declaration block. Where methods have more than two lines they should not be created inline, but should instead be declared as a "prototype" in the class declaration block and defined separately – after the class declaration. The definition must prefix the method name with the class name and the scope resolution operator :: to identify the class containing its prototype.

multiple.cpp

**Don't forget**

Note that a prototype is a statement – so it must end with a semicolon.

**1** Rename a copy of the previous example "object.cpp" as a new program "multiple.cpp"

**2** In the Dog class declaration, replace the three setter methods with a single combined setter prototype that specifies the argument data types – but not their names
**void setValues( int, int, string ) ;**

**3** After the Dog class declaration, add a definition block for the prototype using the :: scope resolution operator to identify the class in which it resides
**void Dog::setValues( int age, int weight, string color )**
**{**

**}**

Notice that, for easy identification, the arguments are named with the same names as the variables to which they will be assigned. Where a class method definition has an argument of the same name as a class member the **this ->** class pointer can be used to explicitly refer to the class member. For example, **this -> age** refers to the class member variable, whereas **age** refers to the argument.

**4** In the method definition block, insert three statements to assign values from passed arguments to class variables

```
this -> age = age ;
this -> weight = weight ;
this -> color = color ;
```

**5** Between the braces of the main method, replace the calls to the three setter methods by a single call to the combined setter method – passing three arguments

```
fido.setValues( 3, 15, "brown" ) ;
```

**6** In the main method, declare a second instance of the Dog class named "pooch"

```
Dog pooch ;
```

**7** Add a second call to the combined setter method – passing three arguments for the new object

```
pooch.setValues( 4, 18, "gray" ) ;
```

**8** Add statements calling each getter method to retrieve the assigned values

```
cout << "Pooch is a " << pooch.getAge() ;
cout << " year old " << pooch.getColor() ;
cout << " dog who weighs " << pooch.getWeight() ;
cout << " pounds ." ;
```

**9** Now add second call to the regular output method

```
pooch.bark() ;
```

**10** Save, compile, and run the program to see the output

**Don't forget**

Where the argument name and class member names are different, the **this ->** class pointer is not needed in the setter method definitions.

```
Command Prompt                                    _ □ ×

C:\MyPrograms>c++ multiple.cpp -o multiple.exe

C:\MyPrograms>multiple
Fido is a brown dog
Fido is 3 years old
Fido weighs 15 pounds
WOOF!
Pooch is a 4 year old gray dog who weighs 18 pounds.WOOF!

C:\MyPrograms>_
```

Fido

Pooch

121

# Initializing class members

Class variable members can be initialized by a special "constructor" method that is called whenever an instance of the class is created. The constructor method is always named exactly as the class name and requires arguments to set the initial value of class variables.

When a constructor method is declared, an associated "destructor" method should also be declared – that is called whenever an instance of the class is destroyed. The destructor method is always named as the class name, prefixed by a ~ tilde character.

Constructor and destructor methods have no return value and are called automatically – they cannot be called explicitly.

Values to initialize class variables are passed to the constructor method in the statement creating an object, in parentheses following the object name.

constructor.cpp

**Hot tip**

The definition of a class method is also known as the method "implementation".

1 Rename a copy of the previous example "multiple.cpp" as a new program "constructor.cpp"

2 In the public section of the Dog class declaration, replace the setValues method prototype with this constructor prototype
**Dog( int, int, string ) ;**

3 Now add an associated destructor prototype
**~Dog() ;**

4 After the Dog class declaration, replace the setValues definition block with a constructor definition block
**Dog::Dog( int age, int weight, string color )**
**{**

**}**

5 In the constructor definition block, insert three statements to assign values from passed arguments to class variables
**this -> age = age ;**
**this -> weight = weight ;**
**this -> color = color ;**

**6** After the constructor definition, add a destructor definition block
**Dog::~Dog()**
**{**

**}**

**7** In the destructor definition, insert a statement to output a confirmation whenever an instance object gets destroyed
**cout << "Object destroyed." << endl ;**

**8** In the main method, edit the statement creating the "fido" object – to pass values to its constructor method
**Dog fido( 3, 15, "brown" ) ;**

**9** Similarly, edit the statement creating the "pooch" object – to pass values to the constructor method
**Dog pooch( 4, 18, "gray" ) ;**

**10** Delete the statements calling the setValues method of the "fido" and "pooch" objects – the constructor has now replaced that method

**11** Save, compile, and run the program – see the output appear as before, plus confirmation when the objects get destroyed

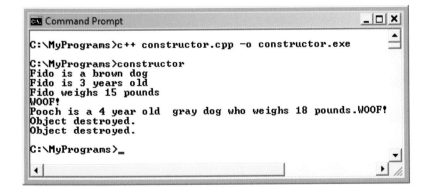

```
Command Prompt                                              _ □ ✗

C:\MyPrograms>c++ constructor.cpp -o constructor.exe

C:\MyPrograms>constructor
Fido is a brown dog
Fido is 3 years old
Fido weighs 15 pounds
WOOF!
Pooch is a 4 year old  gray dog who weighs 18 pounds.WOOF!
Object destroyed.
Object destroyed.

C:\MyPrograms>_
```

**Beware**

The destructor definition begins with the class name "Dog", the scope resolution operator "::", then the destructor method name "~Dog".

**Don't forget**

Although the initial values of the variable members are set by the constructor, setter methods can be added to subsequently change the values – and those new values can be retrieved by the getter methods.

# Overloading methods

Just as C++ allows functions to be overloaded, class methods can be overloaded too – including constructor methods. An overloaded constructor method is useful to assign default values to member variables when an object is created without passing values to the constructor.

overload.cpp

1 Rename a copy of the previous example "constructor.cpp" as a new program "overload.cpp"

2 In the public section of the Dog class declaration, add inline an overloaded bark method – to output a passed string argument when called
**void bark( string noise ) { cout << noise << endl ; }**

3 Now declare a constructor method prototype that takes no arguments (a default constructor method) and an overloaded constructor method prototype that takes two arguments
**Dog() ;**
**Dog( int, int ) ;**

4 After the Dog class declaration, add a definition for the default constructor method – assigning default values to class variables when an object is created without passing any arguments
**Dog::Dog()**
**{**
    **age = 1 ;**
    **weight = 2 ;**
    **color = "black" ;**
**}**

**Don't forget**

The **this ->** pointer is used to explicitly identify class members when arguments have the same name as members.

5 Now add a definition for the overloaded constructor method – assigning default values to class variables when an object is created passing two arguments
**Dog::Dog( int age, int weight )**
**{**
    **this -> age = 1 ;**
    **this -> weight = 2 ;**
    **color = "white" ;**
**}**

6　In the main method, insert a statement to create a Dog object without passing any arguments – calling the default constructor
**Dog rex ;**

7　Add statements calling each getter method to retrieve the default values – set by the default constructor method
**cout << "Rex is a " << rex.getAge() ;**
**cout << " year old "　<< rex.getColor() ;**
**cout << " dog who weighs " << rex.getWeight() ;**
**cout << " pounds ." ;**

8　Now add a call to the overloaded output method
**rex.bark( "GRRR!" ) ;**

9　Insert a statement to create a Dog object passing two arguments – to call the overloaded constructor
**Dog sammy( 2, 6 ) ;**

10　Add statements to retrieve the values set by the overloaded constructor method and call the overloaded output method
**cout << "Sammy is a " << sammy.getAge() ;**
**cout << " year old " << sammy.getColor() ;**
**cout << " dog who weighs " << sammy.getWeight() ;**
**cout << " pounds ." ;**
**sammy.bark( "BOWOW!" ) ;**

11　Save, compile, and run the program

### Beware

Don't add parentheses after the object name when creating an object without passing arguments – notice it's **Dog rex ;** not **Dog rex() ;**.

125

### Hot tip

This is the final rendition of the Dog class. Be sure you can readily identify its public and private members before proceeding.

```
Command Prompt                                    _ □ X
C:\MyPrograms>c++ overload.cpp -o overload.exe

C:\MyPrograms>overload
Fido is a brown dog
Fido is 3 years old
Fido weighs 15 pounds
WOOF!
Pooch is a 4 year old gray dog who weighs 18 pounds.WOOF!
Rex is a 1 year old black dog who weighs 2 pounds.GRRR!
Sammy is a 2 year old white dog who weighs 6 pounds.BOWOW!
Object destroyed.
Object destroyed.
Object destroyed.
Object destroyed.

C:\MyPrograms>_
```

# Inheriting class properties

A C++ class can be created as a brand new class, like those in previous examples, or can be "derived" from an existing class. Importantly, a derived class inherits members of the parent (base) class from which it is derived – in addition to its own members.

The ability to inherit members from a base class allows derived classes to be created that share certain common properties, which have been defined in the base class. For example, a "Polygon" base class may define width and height properties that are common to all polygons. Classes of "Rectangle" and Triangle" could be derived from the Polygon class – inheriting width and height properties, in addition to their own members defining their unique features.

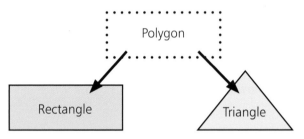

The virtue of inheritance is extremely powerful and is the second principle of Object Oriented Programming (OOP).

A derived class declaration adds a colon : after its class name, followed by an access specifier and the class from which it derives.

derived.cpp

**1** Start a new program by specifying the C++ library classes to include and a namespace prefix to use
```
#include <iostream>
using namespace std ;
```

**2** Declare a class named "Polygon" containing two protected variables, accessible only to members of this class and classes derived from this class, along with a public method to assign values to those variables
```
class Polygon
{
  protected:
    int width, height ;
  public:
    void setValues( int w, int h ) { width = w; height = h ; }
} ;
```

**3** After the Polygon class, declare a Rectangle class that derives from the Polygon class and adds a unique method

```
class Rectangle : public Polygon
{
  public:
    int area() { return ( width * height ) ; }
} ;
```

**4** After the Rectangle class, declare a Triangle class that derives from the Polygon class and adds a unique method

```
class Triangle : public Polygon
{
  public:
    int area() { return (( width * height ) / 2 ) ; }
} ;
```

**5** After the Triangle class, add a main method containing a final return statement and creating an instance of each derived class

```
int main()
{
  Rectangle rect ; Triangle trgl ;
  return 0 ;
}
```

**6** Insert calls to the method inherited from the Polygon base class – to initialize the inherited variables

```
rect.setValues( 4, 5 ) ; trgl.setValues( 4, 5 ) ;
```

**7** Output the value returned by the unique method of each derived class

```
cout << "Rectangle area : " << rect.area() << endl ;
cout << "Triangle area : " << trgl.area() << endl ;
```

**8** Save, compile, and run the program to see the output

**Beware**

Don't confuse class instances and derived classes – an instance is a copy of a class, whereas a derived class is a new class that inherits properties of the base class from which it is derived.

127

**Hot tip**

A class declaration can derive from more than one class. For example, class Box: public A, public B; public C ; .

```
Command Prompt                                    _ □ X

C:\MyPrograms>c++ derived.cpp -o derived.exe

C:\MyPrograms>derived
Rectangle area : 20
Triangle area : 10
```

# Calling base constructors

Although derived classes inherit the members of their parent base class they do not inherit its constructor and destructor. However, it should be noted that the default constructor of the base class is always called when a new object of a derived class is created – and the base class destructor is called when the object gets destroyed. These calls are made in addition to those made to the constructor and destructor methods of the derived class.

The default constructor of the base class has no arguments – but that class may also have overloaded constructors which do. If you prefer to call an overloaded constructor of the base class when a new object of a derived class is created, you can create a matching overloaded constructor in the derived class – having the same number and type of arguments.

basecon.cpp

Son – Parent – Daughter

1. Start a new program by specifying the C++ library classes to include and a namespace prefix to use
   **#include <iostream>**
   **using namespace std ;**

2. Declare a class named "Parent", which will be a base class
   **class Parent**
   **{**
      **// Class members go here.**
   **} ;**

3. Between the braces of the Parent class declaration, insert a public access specifier and add a default constructor to output text – identifying when it has been called
   **public:**
   **Parent()**
   **{ cout << "Default Parent constructor called." ; }**

4. Add an overloaded constructor, which takes a single integer argument, and also outputs identifying text
   **Parent( int a )**
   **{ cout << endl <<**
           **"Overloaded Parent constructor called." ; }**

5. After the Parent class, declare a derived "Daughter" class
   **class Daughter : public Parent**
   **{**

   **} ;**

**6**     In the Daughter class declaration, insert a public access specifier and add a default constructor to output text – identifying when it has been called

```
public :
  Daughter ()
  { cout << endl <<
  "    Derived Daughter class default constructor called." ; }
```

**Beware**

Notice that the syntax in the overloaded Son class constructor passes the integer argument to the overloaded base class constructor.

**7**     After the Daughter class, declare a derived "Son" class

```
class Son : public Parent
{

} ;
```

**8**     In the Son class declaration, insert a public access specifier and add an overloaded constructor which takes a single integer argument, and also outputs identifying text

```
public :
  Son( int a ) : Parent( a )
  { cout << endl <<
  "    Derived Son class overloaded constructor called." ; }
```

**9**     After the Son class, add a main method containing a final return statement and creating an instance of each derived class – calling base class and derived class constructors

```
int main()
{
  Daughter emma ;
  Son andrew(0) ;
  return 0 ;
}
```

**Don't forget**

Each class automatically has an empty default constructor and destructor – for example, Son(){ } and ~Son(){ }.

**10**     Save, compile, and run the program to see the output from each constructor in turn as it gets called

```
Command Prompt                                          _ □ ×
C:\MyPrograms>c++ basecon.cpp -o basecon.exe

C:\MyPrograms>basecon

Default Parent constructor called.
    Derived Daughter class default constructor called.

Overloaded Parent constructor called.
    Derived Son class overloaded constructor called.
```

# Overriding base methods

A method can be declared in a derived class to override a matching method in the base class – if both method declarations have the same name, arguments, and return type. This effectively hides the base class method as it becomes inaccessible unless it is called explicitly, using the :: scope resolution operator for precise identification.

The technique of overriding base class methods must be used with care however, to avoid unintentionally hiding overloaded methods – a single overriding method in a derived class will hide <u>all</u> overloaded methods of that name in the base class!

override.cpp

1. Start a new program by specifying the C++ library classes to include and a namespace prefix to use
```
#include <iostream>
using namespace std ;
```

2. Declare a class named "Man", which will be a base class
```
class Man
{
  // Class members go here.
} ;
```

3. Between the braces of the Man class declaration, insert a public access specifier and an inline output method
```
public :
  void speak() { cout << "Hello! " << endl ; }
```

4. Now insert an overloaded inline output method
```
void speak( string msg )
{ cout << "    " << msg << endl ; }
```

5. After the Man class declaration, declare a class named "Hombre" that is derived from the Man class
```
class Hombre : public Man
{
  // Class members go here.
} ;
```

### Don't forget

The method declaration in the derived class must exactly match that in the base class to override it – including the **const** keyword if it is used.

...cont'd

**6** Between the braces of the Hombre class declaration, insert an access specifier and a method that overrides the overloaded base class method – without a tab output
```
public :
  void speak( string msg ) { cout << msg << endl ; }
```

**7** After the Hombre class declaration, add a main method containing a final return statement and creating two objects – an instance of the base class and an instance of the derived class
```
int main()
{
  Man henry ;
  Hombre enrique ;
  // Add more statements here.
  return 0 ;
}
```

Henry

Enrique

**8** In the main method, insert statements calling both methods of the base class
```
henry.speak() ;
henry.speak( "It's a beautiful evening." ) ;
```

**9** Next insert a statement calling the overriding method in the derived class – producing output without a tab
```
enrique.speak( "Hola!" ) ;
```

**10** Now insert a statement explicitly calling the overridden method in the base class
```
enrique.Man::speak( "Es una tarde hermosa." ) ;
```

**11** Save, compile, and run the program to see the output from the overriding and overridden methods

**Beware**

The overriding method declared in the derived class hides both overloaded classes in the base class. Try calling **enrique.speak()** – the compiler will complain there is no matching method for that call.

# Summary

- The first principle of Object Oriented Programming is the encapsulation of data and functionality within a single class

- Access specifiers **public, private**, and **protected** control the accessibility of class members from outside the class

- A class declaration describes a data structure from which instance objects can be created

- Public setter and getter class methods store and retrieve data from private class variable members

- The scope resolution operator :: can explicitly identify a class

- Class members that have the same name as a passed argument can be explicitly identified by the **this ->** pointer

- A constructor method is called when an object gets created and a destructor method is called when it gets destroyed

- Class variables can be automatically initialized by a constructor

- Class methods can be overloaded like other functions

- The second principle of Object Oriented Programming is the virtue of inheritance that allows derived classes to inherit the properties of their parent base class

- In a derived class declaration the class name is followed by a : colon character, an access specifier, and its base class name

- When an instance object of a derived class is created the default constructor of the base class gets called in addition to the constructor of the derived class

- A derived class method can override a matching method in its base class – also overriding all overloaded methods of that name within the base class

# 8 Harnessing polymorphism

This chapter demonstrates how to separate programs into modular components and introduces the topic of polymorphism – the third principle of Object Oriented Programming.

# Pointing to classes

The three cornerstones of Object Oriented Programming (OOP) are encapsulation, inheritance, and polymorphism. Examples in the previous chapter have demonstrated how data can be encapsulated within a C++ class, and how derived classes inherit the properties of their base class. This chapter introduces the final cornerstone principle of polymorphism.

The term "polymorphism" ( from Greek, meaning "many forms" ) describes the ability to assign a different meaning, or purpose, to an entity according to its context.

In C++, overloaded operators can be described as polymorphic. For example, the * character can represent either the multiply operator or the dereference operator according to its context. Similarly, the + character can represent either the add operator or the concatenate operator according to its context.

More importantly, C++ class methods can also be polymorphic. The key to understanding polymorphism with classes is to recognize that a base class pointer can be created that is also bound to a particular derived class by association.

A pointer to a base class can be assigned the memory address of a derived class to provide a "context" – to uniquely identify that derived class. For example, with a **Base** base class and a derived **Sub** class a pointer can be created like this:

```
Sub inst ;
Base* pSub = &inst ;
```

Don't forget

Turn back to chapter six for more on pointers.

or more simply using the **new** keyword like this:

```
Base* pSub = new Sub ;
```

Where there are multiple derived classes, base class pointers can be created binding each derived class by its unique memory address – which can be revealed using the addressof **&** operator.

classptr.cpp

1    Start a new program by specifying the C++ library classes to include and a namespace prefix to use
```
#include <iostream>
using namespace std ;
```

**2**    Declare a **Base** class containing a method to output a passed integer value in hexadecimal format

```
class Base
{
  public:
  void Identify( int adr ) const
  {
    cout << "Base class called by 0x"
                << hex << adr << endl ;
} ;
```

**Don't forget**

The -> class pointer operator is used here to call class methods.

**3**    Declare two empty derived classes, **SubA** and **SubB**

```
class SubA : public Base {      } ;
class SubB : public Base {      } ;
```

**4**    Declare a main method containing a final return statement

```
int main()
{
  // Program code goes here.
  return 0 ;
}
```

**5**    In the main method, insert statements to create two base class pointers – each binding to a specific derived class

```
Base* ptrA = new SubA ;
Base* ptrB = new SubB ;
```

**6**    Now insert statements that use the pointers to call the base class method, passing the memory address of each for output

```
ptrA -> Identify( (int) &ptrA ) ;
ptrB -> Identify( (int) &ptrB ) ;
```

**7**    Save, compile, and run the program to see the addresses

135

**Hot tip**

The hexadecimal address is passed as an **int** data type then displayed in hexadecimal format by the **hex** output manipulator. The addresses will be different each time the program executes – they are assigned dynamically.

```
C:\MyPrograms>c++ classptr.cpp -o classptr.exe

C:\MyPrograms>classptr
Base class called by 0x22ff54
Base class called by 0x22ff50

C:\MyPrograms>_
```

# Calling a virtual method

A base class pointer that is bound to a specific derived class can be used to call derived class methods that have been inherited from the base class. Methods that are unique to the derived class must, however, be called via an instance object.

A base class pointer that is bound to a specific derived class can also be used to explicitly call a method in the base class using the :: scope resolution operator.

Most usefully, an inherited method in a derived class can override that in the base class when the base method has been declared as a "virtual" method. This is just a regular method declaration in the base class preceded by the **virtual** keyword. The declaration of a virtual method indicates that the class will be used as a base class from which another class will be derived, which may contain a method to override the virtual base method.

virtual.cpp

Beware

Pointers to a base class cannot be used to call non-inherited methods in a derived class.

1. Start a new program by specifying the C++ library classes to include and a namespace prefix to use
```
#include <iostream>
using namespace std ;
```

2. Declare a base class named "Parent" containing a regular method declaration and a virtual method declaration
```
class Parent
{
  public :
    void Common() const
    {    cout << "I am part of this family, " ;    }

    virtual void Identify() const
    {    cout << "I am the parent" << endl ;    }
} ;
```

3. Declare a derived class named "Child" containing a method to override the virtual base method
```
class Child : public Parent
{
  public :
    void Identify() const
    {    cout << "I am the child" << endl ;    }
} ;
```

4 Declare a "Grandchild" class, derived from the "Child" class, containing a method to override the virtual base method and a regular method declaration

```
class Grandchild : public Child
{
  public :
    void Identify() const
    {    cout << "I am the grandchild" << endl ;          }

    void Relate() const
    { cout << "Grandchild has parent and grandparent" ; }
} ;
```

Parent
Child
Grandchild

5 Declare a main method containing a final return statement and creating instances of each derived class, plus base class pointers binding those derived classes

```
int main()
{
  Child son ;
  Grandchild grandson ;
  Parent* ptrChild = &son ;
  Parent* ptrGrandchild = &grandson ;
  // Add more statements here.
  return 0 ;
}
```

137

6 In the main method, insert calls to each method

```
ptrChild -> Common() ;              // Inherited.
ptrChild -> Identify() ;            // Overriding.
ptrGrandchild -> Common() ;         // Inherited.
ptrGrandchild -> Identify() ;       // Overriding.
ptrChild -> Parent::Common() ;      // Explicit.
ptrChild -> Parent::Identify() ;    // Explicit.
grandson.Relate() ;                 // Via instance.
```

Don't forget

Here the Grandchild class inherits the properties of the Child class, which inherits the properties of the Parent class.

7 Save, compile, and run the program to see the output

```
Command Prompt                                    _ □ X
C:\MyPrograms>c++ virtual.cpp -o virtual.exe

C:\MyPrograms>virtual
I am part of this family, I am the child
I am part of this family, I am the grandchild
I am part of this family, I am the parent
Grandchild has parent and grandparent
```

# Directing method calls

The great advantage of polymorphism with multiple derived class objects is that calls to methods of the same name are directed to the appropriate overriding method.

A base class may contain only virtual methods which each derived class may override with their own methods, but base class methods can still be called explicitly using the :: scope resolution operator. This can allow inconsistencies, however – this example would seem to imply that chickens can fly!

birds.cpp

1. Start a new program by specifying the C++ library classes to include and a namespace prefix to use
```
#include <iostream>
using namespace std ;
```

2. Declare a base class named "Bird" containing two virtual method declarations
```
class Bird
{
  public :
    virtual void Talk() const
    { cout << "A bird talks... " << endl ; }

    virtual void Fly() const
    { cout << "A bird flies... " << endl ; }
} ;
```

**Hot tip**

Overriding methods in derived class may, optionally, include the **virtual** prefix – as a reminder it is overriding a base class method.

3. Declare a derived class named "Pigeon" containing two methods to override those in the base class
```
class Pigeon : public Bird
{
  public :
    void Talk() const
    { cout << "Coo! Coo!" << endl ; }

    void Fly() const
    { cout << "A pigeon flies away... " << endl ; }
} ;
```

④ Declare a derived class named "Chicken" containing two methods to override those in the base class

```
class Chicken : public Bird
{
  public :
    void Talk() const
    { cout << "Cluck! Cluck!" << endl ; }

    void Fly() const
    { cout << "I\'m just a chicken – I can\'t fly!" << endl ;
}
} ;
```

Chicken (Bird)
Pigeon (Bird)

⑤ Declare a main method containing a final return statement and creating base class pointers binding derived classes

```
int main()
{
  Bird* pPigeon = new Pigeon ;
  Bird* pChicken = new Chicken ;
  // Add more statements here.
  return 0 ;
}
```

⑥ In the main method, insert calls to each method

```
pPigeon -> Talk() ;
pPigeon -> Fly() ;
pChicken -> Talk() ;
pChicken -> Fly() ;
pPigeon -> Bird::Talk() ;
pChicken -> Bird::Fly() ;          // Inappropriate call.
```

⑦ Save, compile, and run the program to see the output

```
C:\MyPrograms>c++ birds.cpp -o birds.exe

C:\MyPrograms>birds
Coo! Coo!
A pigeon flies away...
Cluck! Cluck!
I'm just a chicken – I can't fly!
A bird talks...
A bird flies...

C:\MyPrograms>_
```

139

Don't forget

The backslash \ character is required to escape the apostrophe in strings.

# Providing capability classes

Classes whose sole purpose is to allow other classes to be derived from them are known as "capability classes" – they provide capabilities to the derived classes.

Capability classes generally contain no data but merely declare a number of virtual methods that can be overridden in their derived classes.

The following example builds upon the previous example to demonstrate how the "Bird" class can be better written as a capability class. Its methods no longer contain output statements but return a **-1** (error) value if they are called explicitly.

It is necessary to change the return type of those methods from **void** to **int** and these changes must also be reflected in each overriding method in the derived classes.

capability.cpp

Don't forget

The return value of overriding methods in derived classes must match those declared in the base class.

1. Start a new program by specifying the C++ library classes to include and a namespace prefix to use
```
#include <iostream>
using namespace std ;
```

2. Declare a base capability class named "Bird" containing two virtual method declarations that will signal an error if called explicitly
```
class Bird
{
  public :
    virtual int Talk() const { return -1 ; }
    virtual int Fly()  const { return -1 ; }
} ;
```

3. Declare a derived class named "Pigeon" containing two methods to override those in the base class
```
class Pigeon : public Bird
{
  public :
    int Talk() const
    { cout << "Coo! Coo!" << endl ; return 0 ; }

    int Fly() const
    { cout << "A pigeon flies away..." << endl ; return 0 ; }
} ;
```

④ Declare a derived class named "Chicken" containing two
methods to override those in the base class

```
class Chicken : public Bird
{
  public :
    int Talk() const
    { cout << "Cluck! Cluck!" << endl ; return 0 ; }

    int Fly() const
    { cout << "I\'m just a chicken – I can\'t fly!"
                                << endl ; return 0; }
} ;
```

Beware

Capability class methods
are intended to be
overridden in derived
classes – they should not
be called explicitly.

⑤ Declare a main method creating base class pointers
binding the derived classes

```
int main()
{
  Bird* pPigeon = new Pigeon ;
  Bird* pChicken = new Chicken ;
}
```

141

⑥ In the main method, insert method calls and a statement
to terminate the program when an error is met by
explicitly calling a base class method

```
pPigeon -> Talk() ;
pChicken -> Talk() ;

pPigeon -> Bird::Talk() ;
if (-1) { cout << "Error! - Program ended."
                                << endl << return 0 ; }

pPigeon -> Fly() ;        // Call will not be made.
pChicken -> Fly() ;       // Call will not be made.
return 0 ;                // Statement will not be executed
```

Hot tip

Refer back to pages 90-
95 for more details on
error handling.

⑦ Save, compile, and run the program to see the output

```
Command Prompt                              _ □ ×

C:\MyPrograms>c++ capability.cpp -o capability.exe

C:\MyPrograms>capability
Coo! Coo!
Cluck! Cluck!
Error! - Program ended.

C:\MyPrograms>_
```

# Making abstract data types

An Abstract Data Type (ADT) represents a concept, rather than a tangible object, and is always the base to other classes. A base class can be made into an ADT by initializing one or more of its methods with zero. These are known as "pure virtual methods" and must always be overridden in derived classes.

adt.cpp

**1** Start a new program by specifying the C++ library classes to include and a namespace prefix to use

```
#include <iostream>
using namespace std ;
```

**2** Declare a base ADT class named "Shape" containing three pure virtual methods

```
class Shape
{
  virtual int getArea() = 0 ;
  virtual int getEdge() = 0 ;
  virtual void Draw() = 0 ;
} ;
```

**3** Declare a derived class named "Rect", containing two private variables

```
class Rect : public Shape
{
  private :
    int height, width ;
} ;
```

**Beware**

It is illegal to create an instance object of an ADT – attempting to do so will simply create a compiler error.

**4** In the derived class declaration, insert a public constructor and destructor

```
public :
  Rect( int initWidth, int initHeight )
  {
    height = initHeight ;
    width = initWidth ;
  }

  ~Rect() ;
```

**5** In the derived "Rect" class declaration, declare three public methods to override the pure virtual methods declared in the "Shape" base class
```
int getArea() { return height * width ) ;
int getEdge() { return ( 2 * height ) + ( 2 * width ) ; }

void Draw()
{
  for( int i = 0 ; i < height ; i++ )
  { for( int j = 0 ; j < width ; j++ ) { cout << "x " ; } }
}
```

Square (Rect)
Quadrilateral (Rect)

**6** Declare a main method containing a final return statement and creating two instances of the derived "Rect" class – to represent a Square and a Quadrilateral shape
```
int main
{
  Shape* pQuad = new Rect( 3, 7 ) ;
  Shape* pSquare = new Rect( 5, 5 ) ;
  // Add more statements here.
  return 0 ;
}
```

**7** In the main method, insert calls to each method then save, compile, and run the program to see the output
```
pQuad -> Draw() ;
cout << "Area is " << pQuad -> getArea() << endl ;
cout << "Perimeter is " << pQuad -> getEdge() << endl ;

pSquare -> Draw() ;
pSquare << "Area is " << pSquare -> getArea() << endl ;
cout << "Perimeter is "<< pSquare -> getEdge() <<endl ;
```

**Don't forget**

A base class need only contain one pure virtual method to create an Abstract Data Type.

```
Command Prompt                                    _ □ ×
C:\MyPrograms>c++ adt.cpp -o adt.exe
C:\MyPrograms>adt
x x x x x x x
x x x x x x x
x x x x x x x
Area is 21
Perimeter is 20

x x x x x
x x x x x
x x x x x
x x x x x
x x x x x
Area is 25
Perimeter is 20
```

# Building complex hierarchies

It is sometimes desirable to derive an ADT from another ADT to construct a complex hierarchy of classes. This provides great flexibility and is perfectly acceptable providing each pure method is defined at some point in a derived class.

hierarchy.cpp

**1** Start a new program by specifying the C++ library classes to include and a namespace prefix to use
```
#include <iostream>
using namespace std ;
```

**2** Declare a base ADT class named "Boat" containing a variable and accessor method together with one pure virtual method
```
class Boat
{
  protected:
    int length ;
  public :
    int getLength() { return length ; }
    virtual void Model() = 0 ;
} ;
```

**3** Declare an ADT class (derived from the Boat class) named "Sailboat" – also containing a variable and accessor method together with one pure virtual method
```
class Sailboat : public Boat
{
  protected :
    int mast ;
  public :
    int getMast() { return mast ; }
    virtual void Boom() = 0 ;
} ;
```

**4** Declare a regular class (derived from the Sailboat class) named "Laser" in which all members will allow public access
```
class Laser : public Sailboat
{
  public :

} ;
```

Don't forget

The Boat class has properties common to any boat whereas the Sailboat class has properties specific to boats that have sails.

144

**5** In the Laser class, insert a call to its constructor method to assign values to the variables in each class from which this class is derived – and call the destructor method
```
Laser() { { mast = 19 ; length = 35 ; }
~Laser() ;
```

Laser
Sailboat (Boat)

**6** In the Laser class, define the pure virtual methods declared in each class from which this class is derived
```
void Model() { cout << "Laser Classic" << endl ; }
void Boom() { cout << "Boom: 14ft" <, endl ; }
```

**7** Declare a main method containing a final return statement and creating an instance of the derived class on the bottom tier of the hierarchy
```
int main()
{
  Laser* pLaser = new Laser ;
  // Add more statements here.
  return 0 ;
}
```

**8** In the main method, insert calls to each defined method
```
pLaser -> Model();
cout << "Length: " <<
        pLaser -> getLength() << "ft" << endl ;
cout << "Height: "<<
        pLaser -> getMast() << "ft" << endl ;
pLaser -> Boom() ;
```

**9** Save, compile, and run the program to see the output

```
Command Prompt                                    _ □ X

C:\MyPrograms>c++ hierarchy.cpp -o hierarchy.exe

C:\MyPrograms>hierarchy

Laser Classic
Length: 35ft
Height: 19ft
Boom: 14ft


C:\MyPrograms>_
```

145

**Hot tip**

Try adding a Powerboat class derived from the Boat class (to contain engine information) and a Cruiser class derived from the Powerboat class – to assign variable values and to define virtual methods.

# Isolating class structures

The source code for each example program in this book is generally contained in a single **.cpp** file to save space but in reality OOP programs are often contained in three separate files:

- Header **.h** file – contains only class declarations

- Implementation **.cpp** file – contains class definitions to implement the methods declared in the header file, which is referenced by an **#include** directive

- Client **.cpp** file – contains a **main** method that employs the class members declared in the header file, which is also referenced by an **#include** directive

For example, a sum calculator program might comprise three files named **ops.h** (a header file declaring operation classes), **ops.cpp** (an implementation file defining the operation methods), and **sum.cpp** (a client file calling the various operations).

When compiling **sum.cpp** the compiler incorporates the included header file and implementation file into the program. It first translates the header file and implementation file into a binary object file (**ops.o**), then it translates the header file and client file into a second binary object file (**sum.o**). Finally, the Linker combines both object files into a single executable file (**sum.exe**).

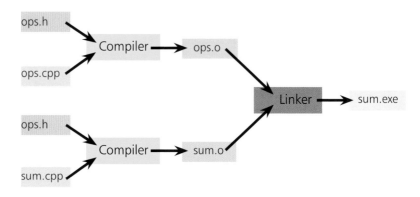

Isolating class structures in separate "modular" files has the advantage of improving portability and makes code maintenance easier by clearly identifying the purpose of each file.

To have the compiler combine all three source code files into a single executable file it is only necessary to explicitly specify the **.cpp** files in the compiler command – an **#include** directive ensures the header file will also be recognized.

For example, with the statement **#include "ops.h"** in both **ops.cpp** and **sum.cpp** the command to compile the example described opposite need not specify the **ops.h** header in the compiler command, but is just **c++ ops.cpp sum.cpp -o sum.exe**.

Calculator

This example will allow the user to input a simple arithmetical expression and output the calculated result. It will provide instructions when first launched and allow the user to make subsequent expressions – or exit by entering a zero character.

1   Start a header file by declaring a class named "Calculator"
```
class Calculator
{

} ;
```

ops.h

2   In the class declaration, insert public method declarations
```
public :
  Calculator() ;        // (Constructor) To set initial status.
  void launch() ;       // To display initial instructions.
  void readInput() ;    // To get expression.
  void writeOutput() ;  // To display result.
  bool run() ;          // (Accessor) To get current status.
```

3   In the class declaration, insert private variable declarations
```
private :
  double num1, num2 ;  // To store input numbers.
  char oper;           // To store input operator.
  bool status ;        // To store current status.
```

Beware

Notice that the header file name must be surrounded by quotes in an **#include** directive – not by the < > angled brackets used to include a standard C++ library.

4   Save the header file as "ops.h"

5   Turn to the next page to continue this example by creating an implementation file – containing definitions for the Calculator class methods declared in the "ops.h" header file

# Employing isolated classes

ops.cpp

**6** Start an implementation file with include directives for the header file created on the previous page and the standard C++ library supporting input/output statements
```
#include "ops.h"          // Reference header file.
#include <iostream>
using namespace std ;
```

**7** Add the following definitions for each method in the header file, then save the implementation file as "ops.cpp"
```
Calculator::Calculator()
{ status = true ; }        // Initialize status.

void Calculator::launch()  // Display instructions.
{
  cout << endl << "*** SUM CALCULATOR ***" << endl ;
  cout << "Enter a number, an operator(+,-,*,/), and
          another number." << endl << "Hit Return to
          calculate. Enter zero to exit." << endl ;
}

void Calculator::readInput()            // Get expression.
{
  cout << "> " ;  cin >> num1 ;         // Get 1st number.
  if( num1 == 0 ) status = false ;      // Exit if it's zero.
  else    { cin >> oper ; cin >> num2 ; }// Or get the rest.
}

void Calculator::writeOutput()          // Display result.
{
  if ( status ) switch( oper )          // If continuing.
  {                                     // Show result.
  case '+' : { cout << (num1 + num2) << endl ; break ; }
  case '-' : { cout << (num1 - num2) << endl ; break ; }
  case '*' : { cout << (num1 * num2) << endl ; break ; }
  case '/' : if( num2 != 0 )
          cout << (num1 / num2) << endl ;
          else cout << "Cannot divide by zero" << endl ;
  }
}

bool Calculator::run()       // Get the current status.
{ return status ; }
```

Beware

Due to space limitation this program makes barely no attempt at input validation – it assumes the user will enter a valid expression, such as 8 * 3.

8 Start a client file with an include directive to incorporate the header file created on page 147
```
#include "ops.h"
```

sum.cpp

9 Declare a main method containing a final return statement and creating a pointer plus a call to display instructions
```
int main()
{
  Calculator* pCalc = new Calculator ;
  pCalc -> launch() ;
  // Add more statements here.
  return 0 ;
}
```

10 In the main method, insert a loop to read expressions and write results while the program status permits
```
while ( pCalc -> run() )
{
  pCalc -> readInput() ;
  pCalc -> writeOutput() ;
}
```

11 Save the client file as "sum.cpp", alongside "ops.h" and "ops.cpp", then compile the program with this command
```
c++ ops.cpp sum.cpp -o sum.exe
```

12 Run the program and enter simple expressions to see the results, then enter zero and hit Return to exit the program

```
Command Prompt                                        _ □ X
C:\MyPrograms>c++ ops.cpp sum.cpp -o sum.exe

C:\MyPrograms>sum

*** SUM CALCULATOR ***
Enter a number, an operator(+,-,*,/), and another number.
Hit Return to calculate. Enter zero to exit.
> 32 + 32
64
> 5.25 - 8.75
-3.5
> 8*3
24
> 20 / 5
4
> 20 / 0
Cannot divide by zero
> 0

C:\MyPrograms>_
```

**Don't forget**

This program loops until the user types a zero and hits Return – changing the "status" control variable to **false**, and so exiting the program.

149

# Summary

- The three cornerstones of Object Oriented Programming are encapsulation, inheritance, and polymorphism

- Polymorphic entities have a different meaning, or purpose, according to their context

- A base class pointer can be used to call inherited methods in the derived class to which it is bound

- A base class pointer can also be used to explicitly call base class methods using the :: scope resolution operator

- Virtual base class methods are intended to be overridden in derived classes

- Polymorphism allows calls to methods of the same name to be directed to the appropriate overriding method

- Capability classes generally contain no data but merely declare virtual methods that can be overridden in derived classes

- Virtual methods that return a **-1** value signal an error to indicate they should not be called directly

- An Abstract Data Type represents a concept and is always the base to other classes

- Declaration of a pure virtual method, with the assignation **=0**, indicates that class is an ADT

- Classes can be derived from an ADT – but you cannot create an instance of an ADT

- An ADT can be derived from another ADT to create a complex hierarchy of classes

- Programs can be separated into header, implementation, and client files to aid portability and to ease code maintenance

- Header files that are referenced by **#include** directives will be automatically included by the compiler during compilation

# 9 Processing macros

*This chapter demonstrates how the C++ compiler can be made to perform useful tasks before compiling a program.*

# Exploring compilation

Whenever the C++ compiler runs, it first calls upon its preprocessor to seek any compiler directives that may be included in the source code. Each of these begin with the **#** hash character and will be implemented first to effectively modify the source code before it is assembled and compiled.

The changes made by compiler directives to the preprocessor create new temporary files that are not normally seen. It is these temporary files that are used to create a binary object file:

- The first temporary file created during compilation expands the original source code by replacing its compiler directives with library code that implements those directives. This text file is named like the source file but with a **.ii** file extension

- The second temporary file created during compilation is a translation of the temporary expanded **.ii** file into low-level Assembly language instructions. This text file is named like the source file but with a **.s** file extension

- The third temporary file created during compilation is a translation of the temporary Assembly language **.s** file into machine code. This binary object file is named like the source file but with a **.o** file extension

**152**

prog.cpp → Compiler → prog.ii → prog.s → prog.o

You can see the temporary files by instructing the compiler to save them using the **-save-temps** compiler option. Both temporary text files can then be examined by opening them in a plain text editor.

Most significantly, you can see that the temporary file with the **.ii** file extension contains the complete function definitions from any included library. For example, it replaces an **#include <iostream>** directive with definitions for the **cin, cout, cerr,** and **clog** functions. The end of the **.ii** file shows the defined functions to be part of the "std" namespace – so they can appear without the **std::** prefix.

**1** Create a simple program named "prog.cpp" that will output a message when it gets executed

```
#include <iostream>
using namespace std ;

int main()
{
  cout << "This is a simple test program" << endl ;
  return 0 ;
}
```

prog.cpp

**2** Issue a command using the **-save-temps** option, to save temporary files, and a **-c** option to compile this program's source files into an object file – with no executable file

**c++ prog.cpp -save-temps -c**

Hot tip

One or more object files can be used to create an executable program – as described on page 146.

**3** Open the .ii file in a plain text editor, such as Notepad, then scroll to the end of the file to see the modified source code – notice how the **<iostream>** library functions are defined in the **std** namespace

153

**4** Open the **.s** file in a plain text editor to see the low-level assembler instructions – notice how the message string is now terminated by the special **\0** character

Hot tip

You can combine these steps, creating an executable file and saving temporary files, by issuing the command
**c++ prog.cpp
-save-temps -o prog.exe**.

**5** Issue a command to output an executable file from the **.o** object file, then run the program to see the message

**c++ prog.o -o prog.exe**

# Defining substitutes

Just as the preprocessor substitutes library code for **#include** directives other preprocessor directives can be used to substitute text or numeric values before assembly and compilation.

The **#define** directive specifies a macro, comprising an identifier name and a string or numeric value, to be substituted by the preprocessor for each occurrence of that macro in the source code.

Like **#include** preprocessor directives, **#define** directives can appear at the start of the source code. As with constant variable names the macro name traditionally uses uppercase, and defined string values should be enclosed within double quotes. For numeric substitutions in expressions the macro name should be enclosed in parentheses to ensure correct precedence.

define.cpp

1. Start a new program by declaring three define directives
```
#define BOOK "C++ Programming in easy steps"
#define NUM 200
#define RULE "********************************"
```

2. Specify the library classes to include and the namespace
```
#include <iostream>
using namespace std ;
```

3. Add a main function containing a final return statement and three statements to output substituted values
```
int main()
{
  cout << RULE << endl << BOOK << endl << RULE ;
  cout << endl << "NUM is: " << NUM << endl ;
  cout << "Double NUM: " << ( ( NUM ) * 2 ) << endl ;
  return 0 ;
}
```

4. Save, compile, and run the program to see the output

**Beware**

Numeric constants are often best declared as **const** variables – because values substituted by the preprocessor are not subject to type-checking.

```
C:\MyPrograms>c++ define.cpp -o define.exe

C:\MyPrograms>define

********************************
C++ Programming in easy steps
********************************
NUM is: 200
Double NUM: 400
```

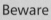

**5** Recompile the program saving the temporary files
**c++ define.cpp -save-temps -o define.exe**

**6** Open the temporary "define.ii" file in a plain text editor
and scroll to the end of the file to see the substitutions

Hot tip

Linux users can employ escaped double quotes \*""string"*\" or plain single quotes *'"string"'* to enclose a quoted string in a command.

```
define.ii - Notepad
File  Edit  Format  View  Help
using namespace std ;

int main()
{
 cout << "********************************" << endl
 << "C++ Programming in easy steps" << endl
 << "********************************" ;

 cout << endl << "NUM is: " << 200 << endl ;

 cout << "Double NUM: " << ((200) * 2) << endl ;

 return 0 ;
}
```

Substitutions can alternatively be made from the command-line
using a **-D***name* option to replace macros with specified values.
Note that string values within double-quotes must also be
enclosed in escaped quotes in the command – so the substitution
will include the double-quote characters.

**7** Delete, or comment-out, the define directives for both the
**BOOK** and **NUM** identifiers – then save the program file to
apply the changes

**8** Recompile the program, specifying substitute macro
values, then run the program once more
**c++ DNUM=50 DBOOK=\""XML in easy steps"\"
define.cpp -o define.exe**

Don't forget

Attempting to compile a program in which an identifier has not been defined will produce a "not declared in this scope" error.

```
Command Prompt                                          _ | □ | ×
C:\MyPrograms>c++ -DNUM=50 -DBOOK=\""XML in easy steps"\"
define.cpp -o define.exe

C:\MyPrograms>define

********************************
XML in easy steps
********************************
NUM is: 50
Double NUM: 100
```

# Defining conditions

The preprocessor can make intelligent insertions to program source code by using macro functions to perform conditional tests. An **#ifdef** directive performs the most common preprocessor function by testing to see if a specified macro has been defined. When the macro <u>has</u> been defined, so the test returns true, the preprocessor will insert all directives, or statements, on subsequent lines up to a corresponding **#endif** directive.

Conversely, an **#ifndef** directive tests to see if a specified macro <u>has not</u> been defined. When that test returns true it will insert all directives, or statements, on subsequent lines up to a corresponding **#endif** directive.

To satisfy either conditional test it should be noted that a **#define** directive need only specify the macro name to define the identifier – it need not specify a value to substitute.

Any previously defined macro can be removed later using the **#undef** directive – so that subsequent **#ifdef** conditional tests fail. The macro can then be redefined by a further **#define** directive:

ifdef.cpp

1. Start a new program with a conditional test to insert a directive when a macro is not already defined
```
#ifndef BOOK
  #define BOOK "C++ Programming in easy steps"
#endif
```

2. Specify the library classes to include and the namespace
```
#include <iostream>
using namespace std ;
```

3. Add a main function containing a final return statement
```
int main()
{
  // Program code goes here.
  return 0 ;
}
```

4. In the main function, add a conditional preprocessor test to insert an output statement when the test succeeds
```
#ifdef BOOK
  cout << BOOK ;
#endif
```

**5**    Add another conditional preprocessor test to both define
a new macro and insert an output statement when the
test succeeds

```
#ifndef AUTHOR
  #define AUTHOR "Mike McGrath"
  cout << " by " << AUTHOR << endl ;
#endif
```

**6**    Next add a conditional test to undefine a macro if it has
already been defined

```
#ifdef BOOK
  #undef BOOK
#endif
```

**7**    Now add a conditional test to redefine a macro if it is no
longer defined and to insert an output statement

```
#ifndef BOOK
  #define BOOK "Linux in easy steps"
  cout << BOOK " by " << AUTHOR << endl ;
#endif
```

**8**    Save, compile, and run the program to see the insertions

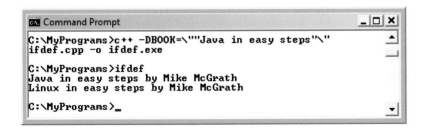

```
Command Prompt                                        _ □ ×

C:\MyPrograms>c++ ifdef.cpp -o ifdef.exe

C:\MyPrograms>ifdef
C++ Programming in easy steps by Mike McGrath
Linux in easy steps by Mike McGrath
```

**9**    Recompile the program, this time defining the **BOOK**
macro in the command, then run the program again to
see the specified value appear in the first line of output

**c++ -DBOOK=\""Java in easy steps"\" ifdef.cpp -o ifdef.exe**

```
Command Prompt                                        _ □ ×

C:\MyPrograms>c++ -DBOOK=\""Java in easy steps"\"
ifdef.cpp -o ifdef.exe

C:\MyPrograms>ifdef
Java in easy steps by Mike McGrath
Linux in easy steps by Mike McGrath

C:\MyPrograms>_
```

**Beware**

Each preprocessor
directive must appear on
its own line – you cannot
put multiple directives on
the same line.

**Don't forget**

On Windows systems
string macro values
specified in a command
must be enclosed in
escaped double quotes.

157

# Providing alternatives

The conditional test performed by **#ifdef** and **#ifndef** can be extended to provide an alternative by adding an **#else** directive. For example:

```
#ifdef WEATHER
  cout << WEATHER ;
#else
  #define WEATHER "Sunny"
#endif
```

Similarly, **#if**, **#else**, and **#elif** macros can perform multiple conditional tests much like the regular C++ **if** and **else** keywords.

For testing multiple definitions the **#ifdef** macro can be expressed as **#if defined** and further tests made by **#elif defined** macros.

While most macros are defined in the source file with a **#define** directive, or on the command line with the **-D** option, some macros are automatically predefined by the compiler. Typically these have names beginning with a double underscore __ to avoid accidental confusion with chosen names. The compiler's predefined macros are platform-specific so a program can employ a multiple definition test to identify the host platform:

1. Launch a plain text editor and save a new file (without any content) as "empty.txt" in your program's directory

2. To see a list of the compiler's predefined macros issue a command calling the cpp preprocessor directly with a "-dM" option on the empty file
   **cpp -dM empty.txt**

3. Scroll through the list to find the "_WIN32" macro on Windows or the "__linux" macro on Linux systems

**Hot tip**

The **#elif** macro simply combines **else** and **if** to offer an alternative test.

else.cpp

**Beware**

Use the **cpp** command to call the preprocessor directly (not the **c++** command) and ensure the **-dM** option is capitalized correctly.

```
Command Prompt                                    _ □ ×
#define __VERSION__ "3.4.5 (mingw special)"
#define _WIN32 1
#define _X86_ 1
#define i386 1
```

```
Terminal                                          _ □ ×
File  Edit  View  Terminal  Tabs  Help
#define __UINTMAX_TYPE__ long long unsigned int
#define __linux 1
#define __unix 1
```

④ Start a new program with a conditional test to seek the
_WIN32 and __linux macros – to identify the platform

```
#if defined _WIN32
  #define PLATFORM "Windows"
#elif defined __linux
  #define PLATFORM "Linux"
#endif
```

⑤ Specify the library classes to include and the namespace

```
#include <iostream>
using namespace std ;
```

⑥ Now add a main function containing a final return
statement and a statement to identify the host platform

```
int main()
{
  cout << PLATFORM << " System" << endl ;
  return 0 ;
}
```

⑦ In the main function, insert statements to execute for
specific platforms

```
if( PLATFORM == "Windows" )
  cout << "Performing Windows-only tasks..." << endl ;
if( PLATFORM == "Linux" )
  cout << "Performing Linux-only tasks..." << endl ;
```

⑧ Save, compile, and run the program to see platform-
specific output

**Beware**

The predefined
**_WIN32** macro has one
underscore but the
**__linux** macro has two
underscore characters.

**Don't forget**

The conditional test of
predefined macros could
be extended to seek
those of other operating
systems and a final **#else**
directive added to specify
an "Unknown" default.

159

# Guarding inclusions

Typically a C++ program will have many **.h** header files and a single **.cpp** implementation file containing the main program. Header files may often contain one or more **#include** directives to make other classes or functions available from other header files and can cause duplication where definitions appear in two files. For example, where a header file includes another header file containing a function definition, the compiler will consider that definition to appear in each file – so compilation will fail.

The popular solution to this problem of re-definition employs preprocessor directives to ensure the compiler will only be exposed to a single definition. These are known as "inclusion guards" and create a unique macro name for each header file. Traditionally the name is an uppercase version of the file name, with the dot changed to an underscore. For example, **RUM_H** for a file **rum.h**.

In creating a macro to guard against duplication an **#ifndef** directive first tests to see if the definition has already been made by another header file included in the same program. If the definition already exists the compiler ignores the duplicate definition, otherwise a **#define** directive will permit the compiler to use the definition in that header file:

add.h

triple.h

guard.cpp

1. Create a header file named "add.h" containing the inline declaration of an "add" function
**inline int add( int x, int y ) { return ( x + y ) ; }**

2. Now create a header file named "triple.h" containing a processor directive to make the add function available for use in the inline declaration of a "triple" function
**#include "add.h"**

 **inline int triple( x ) { return add( x, add( x, x ) ) ; }**

3. Start a new program with preprocessor directives to make both the add and triple functions available
**#include "add.h"**
**#include "triple.h"**

4. Specify the library classes to include and the namespace
**#include <iostream>**
**using namespace std ;**

5 Add a main function containing statements that call both the add and triple functions from the included headers

```cpp
int main()
{
  cout << "9 + 3 = " << add( 9, 3 ) << endl ;
  cout << " 9 x 3 = " << triple( 9 ) << endl ;
  return 0 ;
}
```

**Beware**

Use the conventional naming scheme, where the macro name resembles the file name, to avoid conflicts.

6 Save the files then attempt to compile the program to see compilation fail because the add function appears to be defined twice – in "add.h" and by inclusion in "triple.h"

```
Command Prompt                                    _ □ X

C:\MyPrograms>c++ guard.cpp -o guard.exe
In file included from triple.h:4,
                 from guard.cpp:5:
add.h: In function `int add(int, int)':
add.h:7: error: redefinition of `int add(int, int)'
add.h:7: error: `int add(int, int)' previously defined

C:\MyPrograms>_
```

7 Edit the header file "add.h" to enclose the inline function declaration within a preprocessor inclusion guard

```cpp
#ifndef ADD_H
#define ADD_H

inline int add( int x, int y ) { return ( x + y ) } ;

#endif
```

**Don't forget**

All header files should contain header guards – add a **TRIPLE_H** macro to the **triple.h** file.

8 Save the modified file then compile and run the program – compilation now succeeds because the inclusion guard prevents the apparent re-definition of the add function

```
Command Prompt                                    _ □ X

C:\MyPrograms>c++ guard.cpp -o guard.exe

C:\MyPrograms>guard
9 + 3 = 12
9 x 3 = 27

C:\MyPrograms>_
```

# Using macro functions

The **#define** directive can be used to create macro functions that will be substituted in the source code before compilation.

A preprocessor function declaration comprises a macro name immediately followed by parentheses containing the function's arguments – it is important not to leave any space between the name and the parentheses. The declaration is then followed by the function definition within another set of parentheses. For example, a preprocessor macro function to half an argument looks like this:

**#define HALF( n ) ( n / 2)**

Care should be taken when using macro functions because, unlike regular C++ functions, they do not perform any kind of type checking – so it's quite easy to create a macro that causes errors. For this reason inline functions are usually preferable to macro functions but, because macros directly substitute their code, they avoid the overhead of a function call – so the program runs faster. The resulting difference can be seen in the first temporary file created during the compilation process:

macro.cpp

1. Start a new program by defining two macro functions to manipulate a single argument
   **#define SQUARE( n ) ( n * n )**
   **#define CUBE( n ) ( n * n * n )**

2. After the macro function definitions, specify the library classes to include and a namespace prefix to use
   **#include <iostream>**
   **using namespace std ;**

3. Next declare two inline functions to manipulate a single argument – just like the macro functions defined above
   **inline int square( int n ) { return ( n * n ) ; }**
   **inline int cube( int n ) { return ( n * n * n ) ; }**

4. Add a main function containing a final return statement
   **int main()**
   **{**
      // Program code goes here.
      **return 0 ;**
   **}**

**5** At the start of the main function block, declare and initialize an integer variable
**int num = 5 ;**

**6** Now insert statements to call each macro function and each comparable inline function
**cout << "Macro SQUARE: " << SQUARE( num ) << endl ;**
**cout << "Inline square: " << square( num ) << endl ;**
**cout << "Macro CUBE: " << CUBE( num ) << endl ;**
**cout << "Inline cube: " << cube( num ) << endl ;**

**Hot tip**

Using uppercase for macro names ensures that macro functions will not conflict with regular lowercase function names.

**7** Save the file, then compile the program saving the temporary files and run the program
**c++ macro.cpp -save-temps -o macro.exe**

```
Command Prompt                                    _ □ ×

C:\MyPrograms>c++ macro.cpp -save-temps -o macro.exe

C:\MyPrograms>macro
Macro SQUARE: 25
Inline square: 25
Macro CUBE: 125
Inline cube: 125

C:\MyPrograms>_
```

**8** Open the temporary ".ii" file in a plain text editor, like Notepad, to see that the macro functions have been directly substituted in each output statement

**Don't forget**

An inline function saves the overhead of checking between a function prototype declaration and its definition.

```
macro.ii - Notepad                              □ ⊡ ▣

File  Edit  Format  View  Help

using namespace std ;

inline int square( int n ) { return ( n * n ); }
inline int cube( int n ) { return ( n * n * n ); }

int main()
{
 int num = 5 ;

 cout << "Macro SQUARE: " << ( num * num ) << endl ;
 cout << "Inline square: " << square( num ) << endl ;

 cout << "Macro CUBE: " << ( num * num * num ) << endl ;
 cout << "Inline cube: " << cube( num ) << endl ;

 return 0 ;
}
```

# Building strings

The preprocessor **#** operator is known as the "stringizing" operator as it converts a series of characters passed as a macro argument into a string – adding double quotes to enclose the string.

All whitespace before or after the series of characters passed as a macro argument to the stringizing operator is ignored and multiple spaces between characters is reduced to just one space.

The stringizing operator is useful to pass string values to a preprocessor **#define** directive without needing to surround each string with double quotes.

A macro definition can combine two terms into a single term using the **##** merging operator. Where the combined term is a variable name its value is not expanded by the macro – it simply allows the variable name to be substituted by the macro.

strung.cpp

1. Start a new program by defining a macro to create a string from a series of characters passed as its argument, to substitute in an output statement
**#define LINEOUT( str ) cout << #str << endl**

2. Define a second macro to combine two terms passed as its arguments into a variable name, to substitute in an output statement
**#define GLUEOUT( a, b ) cout << a##b << endl**

3. After the macro definitions, specify the library classes to include and a namespace prefix to use
**#include <string>**
**#include <iostream>**
**using namespace std ;**

4. Add a main function containing a final return statement
**int main()**
**{**
  // Program code goes here.
  **return 0 ;**
**}**

**5** At the start of the main function block, declare and initialize a string variable then append a further string
**string longerline = "They carried a net " ;**
**longerline += "and their hearts were set" ;**

**6** Now add statements to output text using the macros
**LINEOUT(In a bowl to sea went wise men three) ;**
**LINEOUT(On a brilliant night in          June) ;**
**GLUEOUT( longer, line ) ;**
**LINEOUT(On fishing up the moon.) ;**

### Hot tip

Notice that the second statement contains multiple spaces, which will be removed by the stringizing operator.

**7** Save the file, then compile the program saving the temporary files and run the program
**c++ strung.cpp -save-temps -o strung.exe**

```
Command Prompt                                      _ □ ×

C:\MyPrograms>c++ strung.cpp -save-temps -o strung.exe

C:\MyPrograms>strung
In a bowl to sea went wise men three
On a brilliant night in June
They carried a net and their hearts were set
On fishing up the moon.

C:\MyPrograms>_
```

**8** Open the temporary ".ii" file in a plain text editor, like Notepad, to see that the string values and the variable name have been substituted in the output statements

### Don't forget

The merging operator is alternatively known as the "token-pasting" operator as it pastes two "tokens" together.

```
strung.ii - Notepad                              □ ◎ ✕
File  Edit  Format  View  Help

using namespace std ;

int main()
{
 string longerline = "They carried a net " ;
 longerline += "and their hearts were set" ;

 cout << "In a bowl to sea went wise men three" << endl ;
 cout << "On a brilliant night in June" << endl ;
 cout << longerline << endl ;
 cout << "On fishing up the moon." << endl ;

 return 0 ;
}
```

# Debugging assertions

It is sometimes helpful to use preprocessor directives to assist with debugging program code – by defining an **ASSERT** macro function to evaluate a specified condition for a boolean value.

The condition to be evaluated will be passed from the caller as the **ASSERT** function argument. The function can then execute appropriate statements according to the result of the evaluation. Multiple statements can be included in the macro function definition by adding a backslash \ at the end of each line, allowing the definition to continue on the next line.

Numerous statements calling the **ASSERT** function can be added to the program code to monitor a condition as the program proceeds. For example, to check the value of a variable as it changes.

Usefully an **ASSERT** function can be controlled by a **DEBUG** macro. This allows debugging to be easily turned on and off simply by changing the value of the **DEBUG** control macro:

assert.cpp

166

1. Start a new program by defining a DEBUG macro with an "on" value of one – to control an ASSERT function
   **#define DEBUG 1**

2. Next add a macro if-elif statement block to define the ASSERT function according to the control value
   **#if( DEBUG == 1 )**
          *// Definition for "on" goes here.*
   **#elif( DEBUG == 0 )**
          *// Definition for "off" goes here.*
   **#endif**

3. In the top part of the ASSERT function statement block insert a definition for when the debugging control is set to "on" – to output failure details from predefined macros

```
#define ASSERT( expr )                                      \
cout << #expr << " ..." << num ;                            \
if( expr != true )                                          \
{                                                           \
  cout << " Fails in file: " << __FILE__ ;                 \
  cout << " at line: " << __LINE__ << endl ;               \
}                                                           \
else cout << " Succeeds" << endl ;
```

④ In the bottom part of the ASSERT function statement block insert a definition for when the debugging control is set to "off" – to simply output the current variable value

```
#define ASSERT( result )                                    \
cout << "Number is " << num << endl ;
```

⑤ After the macro definitions, specify the library classes to include and a namespace prefix to use

```
#include <iostream>
using namespace std ;
```

⑥ Add a main function containing a final return statement

```
int main()
{
  // Program code goes here.
  return 0 ;
}
```

⑦ At the start of the main function block declare and initialize an integer variable, then call the macro ASSERT function to check its value as it gets incremented

```
int num = 9 ;    ASSERT( num < 10 ) ;
num++ ;          ASSERT( num < 10 ) ;
```

⑧ Save, compile, and run the program to see the output

```
C:\MyPrograms>c++ assert.cpp -o assert.exe

C:\MyPrograms>assert
num < 10 ...9 Succeeds
num < 10 ...10 Fails in file: assert.cpp at line: 36
```

⑨ Edit the program to turn debugging off by changing the control value, then recompile and re-run the program

```
#define DEBUG 0
```

```
C:\MyPrograms>c++ assert.cpp -o assert.exe

C:\MyPrograms>assert
Number is 9
Number is 10
```

**Don't forget**

Predefined macro names are prefixed by a double-underscore and suffixed by a double-underscore.

**Hot tip**

Additionally, the current date and time can be output from the __DATE__ and __TIME__ predefined macros.

167

# Summary

- The C++ compiler's **-save-temps** option saves the temporary files created during the compilation process for examination

- Compilation first writes program code and included library code into a single **.ii** text file, which is then translated into low-level Assembly language as a **.s** text file

- Assembly language **.s** files are translated to machine code as **.o** object files, which are used to create the executable program

- A **#define** directive defines a macro name and a value that the preprocessor should substitute for that name in program code

- The preprocessor can be made to perform conditional tests using **#ifdef**, **#ifndef**, and **#endif** directives

- Preprocessor alternatives can be provided using **#if**, **#else**, and **#elif** directives, and a definition can be removed using **#undef**

- Each header file should use inclusion guards to prevent accidental multiple definition of the same class or function

- The macro name of an inclusion guard is an uppercase version of the file name, but with the dot replaced by an underscore

- A **#define** directive may also define a macro function that will be substituted in program code in place of the macro name

- Inline functions are usually preferable to macro functions because, unlike macro functions, they perform type-checking

- The preprocessor **#** stringizing operator converts a series of characters passed as a macro argument into a string value

- Two terms can be combined into a single term by the preprocessor **##** merging operator

- An **ASSERT** macro function is useful for debugging code and may be controlled by a **DEBUG** macro to easily turn debugging on or off

# 10 Programming visually

*This chapter brings together elements from previous chapters to build a complete C++ application in a visual programming environment.*

# Generating random numbers

The graphical application developed on subsequent pages of this book will generate six random numbers within a specific range. Initially, its functionality can be developed as a console application, then transferred later to illustrate how text-based programming relates to visual programming.

A psuedo-random number from 0.0 to 32,767 can be generated by calling the **rand** function from the C++ **<iostream>** library. The range of generated numbers can be set using the **%** modulus operator to specify a maximum value. For example, to generate a whole number within the range of one to nine:

```
int num = ( rand() % 9 ) + 1 ) ;
```

The numbers generated by **rand** are not truly random, however, as it generates the same sequence each time the program is executed. To generate a different sequence of numbers a "seed" must be specified as an argument to a special **srand** function, such as:

```
srand( 12345 ).
```

Although calls to **rand** will then generate a different sequence of numbers, it is still one that will be repeated each time the program is executed. To generate a changing sequence the argument to **srand** must be something other than a static integer. The solution is to seed the **rand** function using the current time as the argument to **srand,** by calling the **time** function from the standard C++ **<ctime>** library. This returns the time as a **time_t** data type, which can be cast as an integer data type like this:

```
srand( ( int ) time( 0 ) ) ;
```

The **time** function returns the number of seconds elapsed since the epoch at midnight (00:00:00), January 1, 1970, and ensures the numbers generated by **rand** will now appear to be truly random – unless it's called again within the same second.

A series of random numbers generated by **rand** can be used to randomize a consecutive sequence of numbers in array elements. These could represent the range of numbers to choose from when making a lottery selection – and retrieving the value from the required number of arrays could represent a random lottery entry. For example, choosing six numbers between one and 49.

1 Start a new program by specifying the library classes to include and a namespace prefix to use

```cpp
#include <ctime>            // Include time support.
#include <iostream>
using namespace std ;
```

lotto.cpp

2 Add a main function containing a final return statement

```cpp
int main()
{
  // Program code goes here.
  return 0 ;
}
```

3 At the start of the main function block, declare three trivial integer variables and an array for fifty integers

```cpp
int i, j, k, nums[ 50 ] ;
```

4 Seed the random number generator with the current time

```cpp
srand( ( int ) time( 0 ) ) ;
```

5 Fill array elements 1-49 with integers 1-49

```cpp
for( i = 1 ; i < 50 ; i++ ) nums[ i ] = i ;
```

6 Randomize the values in array elements 1-49

```cpp
for( i = 1 ; i < 50 ; i++ )
{
  j = ( rand() % 49 ) + 1 ;
  k = nums[ i ]; nums[ i ]= nums[ j ] ; nums[ j ] = k ;
}
```

Don't forget

You can edit the final loop to output all array elements to see how they are randomized.

7 Now output the values in array elements 1-6

```cpp
cout << "Your six lucky numbers are: " ;
for( i = 1 ; i < 7 ; i++ ) cout << nums[i] << " " ;
```

8 Save, compile, and run the program to see the output

```
Command Prompt                                    _ □ ×
C:\MyPrograms>c++ lotto.cpp -o lotto.exe

C:\MyPrograms>lotto
Your six lucky numbers are: 9  28  7  14  35  45
C:\MyPrograms>lotto
Your six lucky numbers are: 4  46  23  29  11  33
C:\MyPrograms>_
```

# Planning the program

The most widely used visual development environment is the excellent Microsoft® Visual Studio® suite of products. The streamlined Visual C++ Express Edition is a free simplified version for C++ programming and is used throughout the rest of this chapter to demonstrate how to create a graphical application.

When creating a new application it is useful to first spend some time planning its design. Clearly define the program's precise purpose, decide what application functionality will be required, then decide what interface components will be needed.

A plan for a simple application to pick numbers for a lottery entry might look like this:

## Program

- The program will generate a series of six different random numbers in the range 1-49, and have the ability to be reset

## Functionality required

- An initial call to start the random number generator

- A routine to generate and display six different random numbers

- A routine to clear the last series from display

## Components needed

- Six Label controls to display the series of numbers – one number per Label

- One Button control to generate and display the numbers in the Label controls when this Button gets clicked. This Button will not be enabled when the numbers are on display.

- One Button control to clear the numbers on display in the Label controls when this Button gets clicked. This Button will not be enabled when no numbers are on display.

- One PictureBox control to display a static image – just to enhance the appearance of the interface

At the time of writing Visual C++ Express can be downloaded from **www.microsoft.com/express/download**.

---

Hot tip

Toggle the value of the Buttons' Enabled property to steer the user – in this case the application must be reset before a further series of numbers can be generated.

Having established a program plan means you can now create the application basics by adding components to a Form.

1. In Visual C++ Express click File, New, Project and create a new Windows Forms Application named "Lotto"

Hot tip

You can press Shift+F7 to see the Form Designer window at any time.

2. When an empty Form appears in the Form Designer window, click the View, Toolbox menu ( or press Ctrl+Alt+X ) to open the Toolbox window

3. In the Toolbox, expand the Common Controls list then double-click its Label item six times – see six Label controls get added to the Form in the Designer window

4. Now add two Buttons and a PictureBox to the Form

Don't forget

You can alternatively drag items from the Toolbox and drop them onto the Form in the Designer window.

# Assigning static properties

Having created the application basics, on the previous page, you can now assign static values using the Properties window.

**1** Click anywhere on the Form to select it then, in the Properties window, set the Form's Text property to "Lotto Number Generator"

**2** Select the "button1" control then, in the Properties window, change its (Name) property to "getBtn" and its Text property to "Get My Lucky Numbers"

**3** Select the "button2" control then, in the Properties window, change its (Name) property to "resetBtn" and its Text property to "Reset"

**4** Select the "pictureBox1" control on the Form then, in the Properties window, click the column alongside the Image property to see an [...] ellipsis button appear

**5** Click the ellipsis button to launch the Open File dialog then navigate to an illustrative image file and click Open

The image item gets added to the properties window as a System.Drawing. Bitmap object

...and the image now appears in the "pictureBox1" control on the Form

# Designing the interface

Having assigned static property values, on the previous page, you can now design the interface layout.

The size of both the "pictureBox1" control and the "getBtn" control first need to be adjusted to accommodate their content. This can easily be achieved by specifying an AutoSize value so that Visual C++ Express will automatically fit the control neatly around its content.

### Hot tip

You can alternatively use the Smart Tag arrow button on a PictureBox control to set its SizeMode property.

① Select the "pictureBox1" control then, in the Properties window, change its SizeMode property to "AutoSize"

② Select the "getBtn" control then, in the Properties window, set its AutoSize property to "True"

Now you can use the Form Designer's Format menu and Snap Lines to arrange the interface components to your liking

### Beware

Ensure that all PictureBox Margin properties are set to zero if you do not require margins around the image.

③ Hold down the left mouse button and drag around the Labels to select all Label controls

**4** Click Format, Align Tops on the Menu Bar to stack the Labels into a pile

**5** Click Format, Horizontal Spacing, Make Equal to arrange the pile of Labels into a row

**6** Use the Form's right grab handle to extend its width to accommodate the row of Labels and "pictureBox1", then drag the row and both Buttons to top right of the Form

**7** Drag the "pictureBox1" control to top left of the Form, then use the Form's bottom grab handle to adjust its height to match that of the image

177

**8** Use the Snap Lines that appear when you drag controls around the Form to position the row of Labels and the Buttons to make the interface look like this

# Initializing dynamic properties

Having designed the interface, on the previous page, you can now add some functionality to dynamically set the initial Text properties of the Label controls and the initial Button states.

**1** Double-click the Form, or click View, Code on the Menu Bar, or press Ctrl+Alt+0, to open the Code editor

**2** Scroll down the code, to see what you can recognize...

The code begins with a platform-specific **#pragma once** directive, which is an inclusion guard that the Microsoft compiler used by Visual C++ Express understands to mean "only open this file once" during the compilation process.

Of more importance is the **using namespace System;** declaration that comes next – the **System** class namespace provides functions to work with graphical controls, whereas the familiar **std** class namespace provides functions to work with the console.

Code following the namespace declarations defines a derived class named "Form1" whose class members are the interface components and whose class methods are their functions. These can be easily referenced using the familiar **this ->** class pointer.

**3** Near the bottom of the code, locate the empty declaration of the function named "Form1_Load"

**4** Immediately after the closing brace of the Form1_Load function block add a new private "Clear" function – to return a graphical "System::Void" data type
**private: System::Void Clear()**
**{**
  **// Function code goes here.**
**}**

**5** In this new function block, insert statements to set each Label's Text value to an ellipsis when called upon
**this->label1->Text = "..." ;**
**this->label2->Text = "..." ;**
**this->label3->Text = "..." ;**
**this->label4->Text = "..." ;**
**this->label5->Text = "..." ;**
**this->label6->Text = "..." ;**

**Hot tip**

Whenever you type a -> an "Intellisense" window pops up suggesting possible alternatives. Use the up and down keys then hit Enter to choose a suggestion, or press the first letter to skip alphabetically then choose and hit Enter.

**6** Now in the "Form1_Load" function block, insert a call to the new function – to run whenever the Form loads

```
private: System::Void Form1_Load
        ( System::Object^ sender, System::EventArgs^ e )
{
  Clear() ;
}
```

**7** Click the Debug, Start Debugging menu, or press F5, to build the application and see each label name get replaced by an ellipsis when the Form loads

**8** Click the X button to close the window as usual and to stop application debugging in Visual C++ Express

**9** Return to the code window and insert further statements in the Clear function block to control button states

```
this->getBtn->Enabled = true ;
this->resetBtn->Enabled = false ;
```

**10** Press F5 to run the application again and see that the Reset button is now disabled when the Form gets loaded

Hot tip

The ^ character denotes a "handle" reference to a managed System object that has automatic "garbage collection" to prevent memory leaks. Form components are such managed objects.

# Adding runtime functionality

Having created code to initialize dynamic properties, on the previous page, you can now add runtime functionality to respond to clicks on the Buttons.

**1**    In Form Designer, double-click on the **resetBtn** Button control to open the Code Editor in the **resetBtn_Click** event-handler then add this call to the Clear function
**Clear() ;**

This is all that is needed to provide dynamic functionality for the **resetBtn** control. The main dynamic functionality of this application is provided by the **getBtn** control which requires the random number generator to be started when the Form loads. This will require the **srand** and **time** functions so the **<iostream>** and **<ctime>** class libraries need to be included in the program:

**2**    At the start of the program, right after the "pragma once" directive, specify the library classes to include
**#include <iostream>**
**#include <ctime>**

**3**    In Form Designer, double-click on the Form to open the Code Editor in its "Form1_Load" event-handler then insert this code to start the random number generator
**srand( ( int ) time( 0 ) ) ;**

Now you can create the code to provide dynamic functionality for the **getBtn** Button control itself:

**4**    In Form Designer, double-click on the "getBtn" Button control to open the Code Editor in the "getBtn_Click" event-handler then insert this line to declare variables
**int i, j, k, nums[ 50 ] ;**

**5**    In the "getBtn_Click" event-handler, add a loop to fill the "nums" array elements 1-49 with the integer values 1-49
**for( i = 1 ; i < 50 ; i++ ) nums[ i ] = i ;**

**Don't forget**

These steps provide comparable functionality to that of the console application on page 171.

**6** Next in the "getBtn_Click" event-handler, randomize the values in array elements 1-49

```
for( i = 1 ; i < 50 ; i++ )
{
  j = ( rand() % 49 ) + 1 ;
  k = nums[ i ] ; nums[ i ] = nums[ j ] ; nums[ j ] = k ;
}
```

**7** Now in the "getBtn_Click" event-handler, output the values in elements 1-6 to the Form's Label components

```
this->label1->Text = Convert::ToString( nums[1] ) ;
this->label2->Text = Convert::ToString( nums[2] ) ;
this->label3->Text = Convert::ToString( nums[3] ) ;
this->label4->Text = Convert::ToString( nums[4] ) ;
this->label5->Text = Convert::ToString( nums[5] ) ;
this->label6->Text = Convert::ToString( nums[6] ) ;
```

**8** Finally in the "getBtn_Click" event-handler, add these two lines to set the Button states ready to reset the application

```
this->getBtn->Enabled = false ;
this->resetBtn->Enabled = true ;
```

**Hot tip**

The **System::Convert** class provides many functions that make type conversion simple – like the **ToString** function that is used here to convert **int** values to **System::String** values.

181

**Hot tip**

You can click the box buttons in the left margin to expand or collapse function blocks.

```
Form1.h*
Lotto::Form1          getBtn_Click(System::Object ^ sender, System::EventArgs ^ e)

private: System::Void getBtn_Click
              (System::Object^ sender, System::EventArgs^ e)
{
    // Declare trivial variables and integer array.
    int i , j , k, nums[50] ;

    // Fill elements 1-49 with integers 1-49
    for(i=1; i<50;i++) nums[i] = i ;

    // Randomize the values in array elements 1-49.
    for(i=1; i<50;i++)
    {
        j = ( rand() % 49 ) + 1 ;
        k = nums[i] ; nums[i]=nums[j] ; nums[j] = k ;
    }

    // Output the values in array elements 1-6.
    this->label1->Text = Convert::ToString( nums[1] ) ;
    this->label2->Text = Convert::ToString( nums[2] ) ;
    this->label3->Text = Convert::ToString( nums[3] ) ;
    this->label4->Text = Convert::ToString( nums[4] ) ;
    this->label5->Text = Convert::ToString( nums[5] ) ;
    this->label6->Text = Convert::ToString( nums[6] ) ;

    // Set the button states to "Done".
    this->getBtn->Enabled = false;
    this->resetBtn->Enabled = true ;
}
```

# Testing the program

Having worked through the program plan, on the previous pages, the components needed and functionality required have now been added to the application – so it's ready to be tested:

**1** Click the Start Debugging button, or press F5, to run the application and examine its initial appearance

The **Form1_Load** event-handler has set the initial dynamic values of each Label control and disabled the reset button as required.

**2** Click the "getBtn" Button control to execute the instructions within its "getBtn_Click" event-handler

Hot tip

Notice that no number is repeated in any series.

A series of numbers within the desired range is displayed and the Button states have changed as required – a further series of numbers cannot be generated until the application has been reset.

**3** Make a note of the numbers generated in this first series for comparison later

**4** Click the "resetBtn" control to execute the instructions within its "resetBtn_Click" event-handler and see the application resume its initial appearance as required.

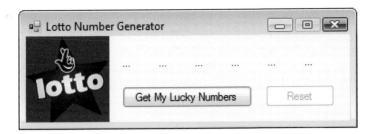

**5** Click the "getBtn" Button control again to execute its "getBtn_Click" event-handler code a second time

Another series of numbers within the desired range is displayed and are different to those in the first series when compared – good, the numbers are being randomized as required.

**6** Click the Stop Debugging button then the Start Debugging button to restart the application and click the "getBtn" Button control once more

The generated numbers in this first series of numbers are different to those noted in the first series the last time the application ran – great, the random number generator is not repeating the same sequence of number series each time the application runs.

**Beware**

Failing to call the **srand** function to seed the Random Number Generator will cause the application to repeat the same sequence each time it runs.

# Deploying the application

Having satisfactorily tested the application, on the previous page, you can now create a stand-alone version that can be distributed to others for deployment elsewhere. There are several ways to do this but the simplest method is to make a "Release" version of the application that can be copied to other machines.

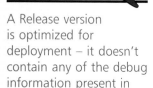
**1** Click the "Solution Configuration" button on the toolbar and choose the Release item from the dropdown list

**2** Click the Build, Build Solution menu, or press F7, to build a Release version of the application, then launch Windows Explorer and navigate to its project directory

**3** The Lotto folder contains the source files, and the Debug folder contains the files created by the Debug version. Double-click the Release folder to find the distributable version of the application

**4** Simply copy the Release file **lotto.exe** to any machine where Visual C++ is installed, then run the application

**5** Now copy the Release file "lotto.exe" to a machine where Visual C++ is <u>not</u> installed to see this error message when you try to run the application:

To run the application the machine needs runtime components of the Visual C++ libraries. These can easily be added using the freely available Microsoft Visual C++ Redistributable package:

**6** In a web browser, visit **www.microsoft.com/downloads** and search for the "Visual C++ Redistributable Package"

**7** The package is available in 32-bit and 64-bit versions – install the appropriate version for the machine, then see that the application can now run successfully:

# Summary

- The C++ **<iostream>** library provides **rand** and **srand** functions that can be used to generate psuedo-random numbers

- Unless first seeded by **srand** the **rand** function will generate the same sequence of numbers each time it is called

- The **time** function provided by the **<ctime>** library can be used to seed **rand** so it appears to generate truly random numbers

- Microsoft Visual C++ Express Edition is a free development environment for visual C++ programming

- A visual program plan should define the program's purpose, required functionality, and interface components needed

- When a new Windows Forms Application project is created in Visual C++ an empty Form appears in Form Designer

- Controls can be dragged from the Toolbox and dropped onto an empty Form, then arranged to construct the interface

- The appearance and performance of any control can be modified by changing its properties

- In visual programming with Visual C++ the **System** class provides functions to work with graphical controls

- Statements can be added to the Form's **Load** function block to dynamically initialize control properties

- Statements can be added to a Button control's **Click** function to provide runtime functionality in response to user actions

- Upon completion a program should be tested to ensure it meets all requirements of the program plan

- The Release version of a program is optimized for deployment

- Visual C++ applications can run on any machine where the runtime components of the Visual C++ libraries are installed

# Index

## Q

## R

## S